MW01174763

Upstream Two
A
Mohawk Valley
Journal

~~~~~~~~~~~~~~~~

A Cultural &
Counter-Cultural
Review

Daniel T. Weaver, Editor

Upstream Publishing
Amsterdam, NY

Dedicated to Ann M. Thane
Mayor of Amsterdam, New York
for her commitment to the Arts

~~~~~~~~~~~~~~~~~

Additional copies of this journal can be ordered at www.thebookhound.net or by sending a check for $11, made out to Daniel Weaver/The Book Hound, to *Upstream* c/o The Book Hound 16 East Main Street Amsterdam, NY 12010.

ISBN-13: 978-1438292052
ISBN-10: 1438292058

~~~~~~~~~~~~~~~~~

Photo Credits. All the photographs in this issue of *Upstream* were taken by Daniel T. Weaver, except for the photos in "From Polish Immigrant to American Citizen" which were taken by John C. Mazur or one of his friends, and any other photo specified otherwise. Unsourced images are in the public domain or covered under the "fair use" clause.

Acknowledgment. A special thanks to Thom Georgia for scanning old photos for this issue of *Upstream.*

Table of Contents

Editor's Note

The first time I met Stephen Lewandowski, a contributor to *Upstream 2*, he asked me why I had decided to focus on Polish-Americans in the Mohawk Valley in the second issue of *Upstream*.

It came about this way. First, I was reading through a book of essays, *Coming and Becoming: Pluralism In New York State History* compiled by Wendell Trip (Cooperstown, NY: New York State Historical Association, 1991), and while it is a good book and contains essays on almost every ethnic group in the state, including some that are quite small, it totally ignores Polish Americans. Then I was going through my entire collection of *Mohawk Valley USA* magazines, a quarterly magazine published from 1980 to1986, and again there was not one mention of Polish-Americans, although there were articles about other ethnic groups.

Then I stumbled upon the novel, *Man's Courage*, by Joseph Vogel, a Polish-American novelist who grew up in Utica. I was impressed with Vogel's skill as a writer. I began researching Vogel and was disturbed by the lack of information about him.

Thomas Napierkowski's, "Does Anyone Know My Name? A History of Polish American Literature," which appeared in the Autumn 2005 issue of *Polish American Studies,* did not mention Vogel at all. A reading of Vogel's *Man's Courage* forces one to at least modify the opening paragraph of Napierkowski's essay which reads:

"Although Polish Americans constitute one of the largest immigrant/ethnic groups in the United States, their standing in the world of American literature is rather unflattering. For one thing, their image in American literature of critical acclaim and national circulation, especially in the middle of the twentieth century, was grim indeed; and most people, including many Polish Americans, would have been hard pressed during that period to name even one or two major authors of Polish American origin. These circumstances have caused serious problems for Polonia."

There is also, of course, the poet and novelist, Charles Bukowski, and Isaac Bashevis Singer. Singer, like Vogel, muddies the waters a bit because he is not only Polish but also Jewish. Napierkowski believes that Singer would reject the idea that he was a Polish-American writer.

In her book, *Traitors and True Poles*, Karen Majewski reveals just how rich the storehouse of Polish-American literature is. But it was mostly written in Polish, which most Americans cannot read, even many Americans of Polish descent.

I don't know that I had ever met a Polish-American until I moved to Amsterdam, NY, a city with a large Polish community, in 1978. The mayor of Amsterdam at the time, John Gomulka, was Polish.

One of my first jobs in Amsterdam was as a night watchman in the Coleco Toy Factory. One night I was working with Gene Bojanowski, and we started talking about World War 2. Rolling up his pant leg, he showed me scars from dogs that the Germans purposely set upon him when he was incarcerated in a concentration camp. The only thing that saved his life in that camp was his American citizenship. He had been born in the USA, but his parents had returned to Poland when he was a child. From Gene and others I learned about Polish suffering in World War 2.

For many years I bought into the Bieganski stereotype of Poles and Polish Americans—dumb brutes, half human and half animal—that Danusha Goska writes about in her book, *Bieganski*. I laughed when people told Polish jokes. Indeed, one of the most insidious aspects of ethnic jokes is that they are almost always funny.

The 1970s television show, *All in the Family*, a liberal show whose stated purpose was to destroy stereotypes, failed miserably for the most part. When you give the best lines to the best actor in the show, Carroll O'Connor, you make it possible for a racist to watch and enjoy the show. And when you make the Polish-American son-in-law, played by Rob Reiner, the butt of those jokes, when you give him trite moralistic lines that are neither funny nor powerful, when you allow the best actor on the show to call him Polack and Meathead, you end up reinforcing rather than destroying stereotypes of Polish-Americans.

Rarely did Mike Stivic get the best of Archie Bunker. On the other hand, Lionel, the African-American neighbor, always got the best of Archie, which must have been very empowering for African-Americans who watched the show. But the show only set in stone what many of us already believed to be true about Poles and Polish-Americans.

Coming to know many Polish-Americans in the Mohawk Valley who did not fit the Bieganski stereotype was helpful in gaining an appreciation of Poles and Polish-Americans. When I went to work at the Post Office in Amsterdam, Ed Czynokowski was the only other employee who shared my literary and cultural interests. Chester Jezierski, Jr., an engineer at GE, has been my brother-in-law for thirty years now. The legacies of Lech Walesa and Pope John Paul II also helped. So did reading Jan Karski's autobiography and Linda Wisniewski's memoir, *Off Kilter. A Woman's Journey To Peace With Scoliosis, Her Mother & Her Polish Heritage*. (See Linda's interview with former Lt. Governor, Mary Ann Krupsak in this issue of *Upstream*). And the many articles, essays and poems by Polish-Americans in *Upstream 2* reveal the breadth and depth of Polish-American contributions to our cultural life.

Of course, not every article in this issue is related to Polonia. Donna Reston's article on a Schoharie County folk artist whom she discovered is just one of many wonderful additions to *Upstream 2*. See the front cover for a sample of his work. And as usual, we have not shied away from taking on controversial issues.

I was pleased with the first issue of *Upstream*. Constructive criticism from several readers resulted in minor changes in this issue. There was a lot of criticism of the aesthetics of the journal's interior. However, we believe that readability, black 12 point type on a white background, a clean look, easy on the eyes, is important. Many journals today suffer from the influence of MTV, Twitter and Facebook—tidbits of information strewn across the page with lots of photos. The effect may be artistic, but, for me at least, it is not conducive to reading. I believe the content of this issue is stronger than the first one, and that's what counts. I hope you find that true also.

Claude L. Mann: "He Was an Artist, You Know"

by Donna L. Reston

Who would have thought that five unsigned oil paintings on canvas, stripped from their stretchers, stuck together, and stored in an attic trunk for many years, would have served as my passport on a journey to discover an almost lost American folk artist?

My introduction to Claude L. Mann (1883-1959) started with a house call. I am an antiques dealer specializing in books and paintings, and one day I received a call from a couple preparing to move to Arizona. The books that I had been called to purchase were in poor condition and not of interest to me, so I asked about other items that might be for sale. The gentleman took me out to his garage, where I got my first glimpse of Mann's work.

Despite the deplorable condition of these paintings, I was excited by the vibrant colors, the subject matter, and the vitality of the work. After I paid for them, the owner was kind enough to tell me that he had purchased them some ten years earlier at a barn sale in Schoharie, New York, and described to me where the property was located. From that information, I was able to discover who had lived in the house at that time and to track down the elderly woman who had held the barn sale and since moved to Texas.

After many long-distance phone calls, I was still not certain who had painted these intriguing pictures until I contacted an old friend of mine, Donald Duell, professor emeritus at the State University of New York at Cobleskill and a fellow folk art enthusiast. When I described the work to him over the phone, he told me that he had seen a similar work some years earlier at a small art show held at the library in Cobleskill, New York, and he had a photo.

Immediately I jumped into my car and, 45 minutes later, was in Don's driveway. As soon as I saw the photo, I knew it was the same hand. And it was clearly signed "C.L. Mann." The rest, as they say, is history, and my journey had a destination.

We learned that Mann had lived in the village of Beards Hollow, and Don and I started an intensive search to locate other paintings and to interview several people who might remember Mann, either as children or as neighbors. We were even able to locate and to talk with the woman who had owned the nursing home where Mann spent the last 11 years of his life and where he painted until about a year before he died. She unwittingly supplied the title for this article. When she was asked if she remembered Claude Mann, her immediate and unprompted response was, "He was an artist, you know."

Mann painted in three distinct styles. His earliest works, in both oil and watercolor, have almost a miniature quality about them-tiny buildings and figures blended into a meticulously rendered landscape. His works when, as Don said, he was at the "peak of his powers," are larger, bolder, and more graphic. His last works, painted after entering the nursing home and when he suffered from arthritis in his hands, are still striking but much less detailed; these works depict fewer people.

Mann lived on farmland that had been in his family since the 19th century. Many members of the Mann family are recorded in Roscoe's *History of Schoharie County*. They farmed, operated sawmills and taverns, and held various local political offices. They also became fairly large landowners.
Mann is listed in several early census records as a farm laborer. He often entertained neighborhood children at his farm by giving them free pony rides and allowing them to watch him train the animals, an activity that sometimes took place in the summer kitchen of his home in a specially constructed ring. It was also in this room that he did his painting, standing at a bench littered with paints, his subject those same ponies. Visitors remember many paintings of horses tacked onto the walls of this room.

At some time in his life-probably after the sudden death of his wife and his father in 1936-he must have begun to reflect upon his life in the hollow, a life that had been the source of so much joy. He seems to have made a deliberate decision to record that life. Moreover, despite the tragic and untimely death of his wife from peritonitis, beginning what must have been a painfully lonely period in his life, the paintings of this period show a joyful and even at times an unexpectedly humorous nature. Painting a cow lifting its tail, or a sheep scratching its nose, or, on the reverse side of *Threshing Buckwheat*, an unfinished and somewhat risqué oil sketch of Adam and Eve holding hands and dancing in an idyllic landscape with two deer watching, Mann demonstrated that he had a sense of humor and a delight in life.

Mann might also have been stimulated to paint local farm life after having read several books written by the Reverend John Van Schaick during the 1920's and 1930's, which idealized the tiny community and landscape of Beards Hollow. Van Schaick was a prominent Universalist minister who, in 1914, when he first took over the family property in the hollow as a summer residence, had married Claude and Edna. *The Shivaree* might well represent Mann's own marriage, probably in Van Schaick's home.

A prominent churchman, Reverend Van Schaick traveled between Washington, D.C., and Boston and played a prominent role heading Red Cross relief to Belgium during World War I. But he and his wife always came back to the hollow for respite, which also provided him with an opportunity to pursue his interests in nature and in ornithology. Sometime in the 1930's, he took over Sunday services in the tiny Beards Hollow church. Although Mann was not a churchgoer, his wife, Edna, attended and played the church organ.

Mann might also have found inspiration in Depression era efforts to recall and memorialize "the old days." It was a time when government sponsored the writing of state histories and set artists to work painting murals in public buildings. There is no evidence that Mann ever participated in any such public projects; his farm activities and pony-raising would not have left much time for that. But he did paint in his spare moments-constantly, it would seem from our interviews.

Mann exercised a certain artistic license when he portrayed the buildings of Beards Hollow. Even the church, which he painted at least twice, sports an extra window. The house in *The Bees Are Swarming* exhibits nonexistent dormers. The house in *The Shivaree* is probably a compilation of the features of several different homes along Beards Hollow Road.

His attention to facial detail in painting the figures in his pictures has led me to conclude that he had at least some of his actual neighbors in mind. Reverend Van Schaik's nephew thought that the large man firing the gun next to the house in *The Shivaree* might possibly be "Tiny" Mattice, Mann's brother-in-law. We also know that Mann painted himself in at least three of the paintings we have located.

Although we have no actual photo of the artist, we do have physical descriptions by people who knew him, including the woman who ran the nursing home where he died. He was described as balding with a shock of white hair; he also wore red suspenders and didn't wear socks. He stands prominently in the foreground of The Shivaree holding a cane.

Even now, my journey is unfinished, but I welcome others to join me. My itinerary includes the publication of a book about Claude L. Mann. Should anyone have any of his paintings or any information to share with me, I would be most appreciative.

You may contact me at (518) 843-1601.

Donna Reston is a retired high school American History teacher and has been an antique enthusiast since a teenager. She has operated Reston Books & Antiques since 1979. A special interest is folk art paintings by 18th to early 20th Century New York State artists.

Clarissa Putman - Fact Rather Than Fiction

Peter Betz, Fulton County Historian

Many years ago, a visitor arrived at Johnson Hall just at closing time. Then Superintendent Col. Charles Briggs, being retired military, was not inclined to remain open for a late arriver, but, to hear him relate the story - and I and others did - he made an exception when the woman explained her motive: she could not come back tomorrow, she explained but she did not expect Col. Briggs to give her a full tour of the hall after closing time. "I just want to walk inside the front door of this house that my great, great, great grandmother wasn't good enough to live in. My name is Clarissa Putman."

As a student of Johnson family history, Briggs knew instantly what the young woman meant: somehow, she must be a descendant of that colonial-era Clarissa Putman, the first and probably only real love of Sir John Johnson, and the mother of his first two children, Margaret and William.

When Sir William Johnson got off the ship that brought him to America he was plain William Johnson, 23 years old. By 1770, nobody was about to remind him of his fairly-humble beginnings, but he was reminded every day himself by his various debilitating ailments that he could not purchase immortality. He could, however assure himself his family name would continue. His son John had already been busy following in his father's noted procreational footsteps: with the cooperation of a healthy younger Dutch girl from Tribes Hill - Clarissa Putman - he produced a son and daughter and some say, allowed this unofficial family to reside with him at Fort Johnson. This was good practice, but in Sir William's mind, it didn't count, because John was more than just his father's son: he was also the key to securing future generations of this new-world Johnson dynasty, but not - at his station in life - through an ordinary valley girl.

Sir John Johnson

Perhaps Sir William at this point suffered his own buyer's remorse: his consort, Sir John's mother, was Catherine Weisenberg, a runaway indentured immigrant. This social blemish could be politely forgotten by Anglo-American society in lieu of Johnson's later accomplishments, but there could be no room in the upper-class ballrooms and political offices he envisioned his son would travel, for another poor, uncultured female to be part of the official Johnson family. Sir John, Sir William decreed, must be sent to New York to appropriate for his legal consort a cultured young woman from an acceptable upper-class, wealthy, politically-influential family with whom to co-produce an official family - the next generation of empirecontinuers. And for that to happen, Sir John's unofficial first family must be swept aside.

The ironic mistake in Sir William's myopic thinking was that Clarissa Putman - of whom he thought so little, and of whom there is not a single mention in his voluminous communications - was herself a fifth generation American whose original ancestor arrived here decades before him!

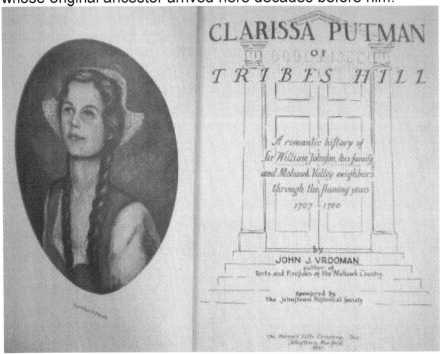

Clarissa Putman first came to my attention when I purchased *Clarissa Putman of Tribes Hill*, a lengthy book written by John Vrooman, for my father as a Christmas present. On October 22nd, 1952 the *Oswego Palladium-Times* reprinted an entire speech given by Vrooman on the subject of researching for his book. Vrooman candidly recounted his failed attempt to interview a 94 year-old Putman descendant of Clarissa's brother Victor, who claimed she had never heard of Clarissa, thereby irritating Vrooman who declared, "I still incline to the belief that she knew a great deal but she carried it to the grave with her a few months later." Vrooman tried to get it right, researching the Claus Papers and interviewing current Baronet Sir Gordon Johnson. He had little choice but to either quit or weave a story part fact, part fiction. As he told the Oswegoans, "A factual biography of Clarissa is impossible. She is far too shadowy a figure across the pages of history."

19th century historian Jeptha Simms in 1850 interviewed several elderly Schenectady women and related that "These ladies were all acquainted with Miss Putman and greatly respected her." They would have known her in the early 19th century, when she was reputedly one of Schenectady's best dress-makers.

What frustrated John Vrooman and frustrates researchers today are the gaps. We can only guess at her whereabouts or her living circumstances after Sir John bowed to his father's will and cast her aside, nor help wonder where she and the children were during Sir John's 1780 raids. Her father Arent's property is generally described as being at Tribes Hill, but he owned land on both sides of the river, and his main establishment seems to have been on the south, beneath that high ridge looking down on Fort Hunter, known as Coughdaurity. Did she ever really occupy that lonely little cabin known as the Putman House, still standing roughly across the river from St. Mary's Hospital, and if so, how did she acquire it?

When did she return to Schenectady, the home of her direct Dutch ancestors, where she spent the last forty-some years of her life? Questions like these can be answered in a general way, but not with certitude.

Clarissa Putman's father was Arent Victor Putman, baptized at the Schenectady Dutch Reformed Church, February 14th, 1719. Arent received his Mohawk Valley property from their father Victor in a division of land between himself, three brothers and one sister. Victor was likely a Schenectady merchant/Indian trader who purchased land lying between Fort Johnson and Fonda on both sides of the Mohawk. On August 5th, 1743, Arent married Elizabeth, daughter of Jacob and Margaret (Van Slyke) Peek. They were living in or near Caughnawaga (Fonda) in 1764. Ironically, wherever they were living on the morning of May 2nd, 1780 during Sir John's raid, Arent Putman was killed, perhaps by the same raiding party that attacked Colonel Visscher's family and later murdered old Douw Fonda, one of his father's earliest mentors.

But that would come later. While the Johnson Papers give a fairly clear picture of Sir William's activities, Sir John's are less clear. From mid 1763, when his father occupied Johnson Hall, Sir John lived in and managed the 600 acre farm at Fort Johnson. Just when in the 1760's John and Clarissa began their romance will never be known. No long-lost diary or stash of secret love letters will ever be discovered, but there is no reason not to think they crossed paths many times while she was maturing. Clarissa's parents frequently traded at Robert Adem's Johnstown store, but in the trading-ledger, there is only one mention of Clarissa. In fact, it may not be her at all, since Arent had several daughters, but on August 11th, 1769 "Arent Potman & daughter" purchased 6 yards of black fabric, one and a half dozen buttons, and silk trimmings. Someone was going to make a dress, and of course Clarissa is known to have supported herself successfully as a seamstress after moving to Schenectady.

In this study of the relationship between Sir John Johnson and Clarissa Putman, we must apply a little (very) fuzzy math. Sir John was born November 5th, 1742. Cornelia Clarissa Putman was born January 29, 1751. Astrologically, this combination of Scorpio male and Capricorn female is fairly homogenous. To quote one authority, "Because the Scorpio possesses an inherent need to establish a peaceful, quiet life to settle with, he or she may very likely be drawn to a Capricorn who is particularly known for being serious, pragmatic and well reserved in every way." Birthdates on the children vary from source to source. Most suggest daughter Margaret was born during 1766, but if so, this birth occurred when Sir John was already in England, having left America around October 1st, 1765. If he left Clarissa pregnant behind him, probable birth dates for Margaret would center around mid 66. Sir John returned about the end of August, 1767 and son William was born during 1770, suggesting they resumed their relationship upon his return from Europe. But if these fuzzy dates are correct, Margaret was born when Clarissa was not yet sixteen.

Whether Clarissa understood his motive or not, Sir John left for New York in the fall of 1771, obeying his father's admonition to examine available society ladies for a suitable wife, suitable meaning from an old, established, wealthy, politically-connected family. On this first shopping trip, the diffident John stayed only several weeks, to little effect. As Sir William recalled in a letter to John Blackburn, May 28th, 1772, "He spent but a few weeks last fall in New York and has not come to any determination in favor of any matrimonial scheme. Whenever he enters into that state, it will afford me much pleasure, as I am thoroughly sensible that he ought to do so, though I would lay no force on a young man's inclinations." Clearly, in Sir William's mind, Clarissa and her children, even one given his own name, had no status and could expect no recognition of legitimacy.

Sir John returned to New York to try again late in the fall of 1772, and this time remained a considerable time. On February 10th, 1773 Guy Johnson wrote from New York regarding the success of Sir John's second 'hunting trip', declaring "he will return with me and doubtless lay before you the final determination of the family here respecting his union, which I see nothing to prevent." The proposed union was with Mary "Polly" Watts, a daughter of John Watts, a wealthy and prominent merchant/land-owner and political ally of Sir William. Sir William was quite satisfied, writing to Thomas Moncrieffe in March that he had "long desired to see him happily settled." Again, Sir John's happy settlement, in his father's eyes, was not to be conducted with a valley Dutch girl.

LADY JOHNSON.

When we speak of Clarissa Putman, there is so much more we don't know than what we do. When and with what emotions did she give way to the new order of things, and for that matter, where did she reside from the time John returned from New York and announced his engagement? The old valley legend that she and the children vacated Fort Johnson and took up living at the still-standing Putman House on the other side of the river sometime around late 1771 may well be true, but if so, history is silent about it, and there are questions about the house. We do know she enrolled both children in a school at Tribes Hill, but that is some miles from the Putman

House, and since both her father and brothers had farms and business ventures in the immediate Fort Hunter/Tribes Hill area, wouldn't she have settled there among them?

Clarissa Putman House on Yankee Hill, 2012.

When the revolution ended and the dust settled, as early as 1784 Sir John re-engaged in communication with Clarissa via a trusted go-between, Schenectady merchant Daniel Campbell. Campbell at that time informed Sir John he was engaged in convincing Clarissa to bring her children to Schenectady to continue their education.

By 1786 he succeeded. She was already living in Schenectady when Campbell wrote Sir John, "I have had some conversation with Clara about a house and if she liked the one she now lives in, but could draw nothing from her to express any desire to have one purchased for her, although it is not of much consequence for such an act of your generosity would make her completely happy." Some conversation indeed, since Campbell is being coy with Sir John: Campbell well-knew, because he must have engineered it, that Clarissa had already moved into two rooms in the house right next door to his, and probably with his assistance, already began her life-long occupation as "mantelmaker". Regarding acquiring a house, it sounds as if, in her independent Dutch way, she was telling both men, "I can do it myself, thank you."

Also, regarding the Putman House, past archaeological digs reveal evidence of burned materials at a certain earth stratum, suggesting the presence and destruction of an earlier house at that site, very likely during the 1780 raids. Thus the present house, while very early, is most likely the second one at that location. Where Clarissa was while such a conflagration occurred, perhaps hiding in the woods like everyone else while her former lover's Indian and Tory bands burned down her house, can only be guessed at. The fuzzy math, based on fuzzy facts, only suggests Clarissa and the children could have resided in the original house from early 1772 until October, 1780, and in the present home (built over the ruins of the first), until circa 1785 when she definitely moved to Schenectady.

Meanwhile back at the fort and the year 1772, preparing Fort Johnson to become a suitable home for a New York society bride cost Sir William, who stood good for it, almost 500 pounds. Sir John and Lady Mary were married in New York, June 29th, 1773. John Watts wrote Sir William to expect them adding, "God bless them both and make them long happy, the prospect is certainly fair," and fair it was, since no one could have foreseen that within almost exactly three years, Sir William would be dead, Sir John would be eating roots on his flight to Canada, Johnson Hall would be abandoned and vandalized, all Johnson family property seized, and John's "proper" high-society bride and children would be in Albany, held under guard by members of a new government. Wherever Clarissa was, she, like virtually all the Mohawk Valley Dutch, embraced the patriot cause and had no problem keeping their property.

Unanswerable questions continue. To what extent after his "proper" marriage did Sir John continually provide for Clarissa? Did she go home to her Tribes Hill family or to the isolated little home on the south side of the river? Perhaps most interesting, did he sometimes, before being forced the flee the valley, saddle up to go riding, and, unknown to Polly, end up making clandestine journeys to wherever Priscilla and the children were residing to visit his other family?

I can relate only what we do know, which comes from a letter written to Sir John by Daniel Campbell the 9th of August, 1784. Early under suspicion because of his strong connections with the Johnson's, Campbell, perhaps because of his connections and management skills in the locating and transporting mercantile goods, survived safety committee suspicions, proved useful to the cause, and greatly prospered.

Second Floor Bedroom, Clarissa Putman House, Yankee Hill. 2012.

In this letter Campbell informs Sir John that Clarissa has finally brought William and Margaret to Schenectady to attend school there. Campbell advanced her money to buy clothes for them and to rent the two rooms next to his home. It was her intention, he informed John, to turn her skill as a seamstress into a permanent trade. Campbell assured John "she is very industrious and behaves with a good character." He also reminded Sir John she had already seen to it the children attended the school at Tribes Hill.

Fast forward to 1786. Back from a long, necessary trip to England pursuing his loyalist claim, Sir John resumed his long-distance involvement with Clarissa and the children. In more letters traveling via Daniel Campbell, he urged Clarissa to allow William to come to Niagara and she eventually agreed. A bargaining chip may have been his instruction to Campbell to find her a decent house if she wanted one, this being the first mention of a house. Money was sent Campbell to outfit William for the trip and someone reliable to accompany him was found.

William arrived May 22nd and was placed in the care of Dr. John Dease, Sir William's nephew and former doctor.

Meanwhile in Schenectady, Campbell was instructed to see Peggy educated at proper schools. Campbell informed Sir John that she "wrote with a good hand" and was advanced in arithmetic. From time to time, Campbell sent Sir John specimens of her hand-writing and transmitted money sent for her school bills.

In early 1788, Sir John wrote Clarissa and asked her to send Margaret to Niagara. This time, Clarissa refused. When Campbell heard of it, he asked Clarissa why she hadn't agreed. She replied it was simply too hard to part with both children. Campbell then artfully proposed to both of them that they send Peggy to a new Schenectady dancing school. "The man teaches wale (well) my son goes to him." Sir John agreed to pay for this. Some time later, Campbell wrote Sir John that, "I really think she is much improved and if she is properly taken care of will make so fine a young lady."

Apparently she did well, for early in 1792, Daniel Campbell wrote Sir John that Margaret had married James Van Horne of the industrious Dutch Van Horne family. Young Van Horne, a son of the founder of Van Hornesville, was represented by Campbell as being "industrious, sober and well-behaved. he is really a very good young man and of suitable age to her." The couple had respectfully written for Sir John's permission, but having not heard from him, they went forward with the nuptials. When he finally received the news, Sir John returned his congratulations and offered to set up his new American son-in-law in the Indian trade, but the young man replied politely that, while he appreciated the offer, he did not wish to give up his present business which was beginning to prosper. Indeed, Schenectady was a far better place to be located than in a lean-to at some frontier outpost.

On the 10th of March, 1800, in far away Canada, Sir John, perhaps honoring a request, wrote Margaret giving her family permission to occupy his father's personal church pew at Schenectady's St. George's Episcopal Church. "To Whom It May Concern: I hereby relinquish and give over to Mrs. Van Horne of Schenectady, all my Right, Title or Claim to the Pew formerly (illegible) in the English churc(h) for my father and afterwards occupied by myself. Given under my hand at Montreal the 10th day of March 1800. John Johnson"

The years rolled onward. Sir John remained in Canada, dutifully but rather unhappily, with wife Polly. It was no longer a happy union. Hardly any extant letters issued from either's pen to personal friends does not contain complaints about the other. Clarissa prospered as one of Schenectady's most in-demand dress-makers while Sir John executed his duties as Indian Superintendent, bought and sold properties, made frequent, unwanted trips to England to please his socially-conscious wife, but a gradual, irreconcilable separation broadened between them. Polly summed it up in a September 14th, 1809 letter to her brother. "We do not agree on any one subject and not only that, but every disrespect and improper language is used to me. I was in hopes that the years would have made some changes". No doubt Polly shared some of the blame. Perhaps she was not perceptive enough to realize that, as he grew older, Sir John more and more frequently lost himself in bitter thoughts and memories of the beautiful empire his Loyalism cost him, the beautiful mansion, the carriages and finery, the respect, and the woman his father's ambitions for him forced him to leave behind in another country.

But when the wife goes away, sometimes the knight will play. In the summer of 1809, after Lady Polly left on yet another trip to England, a later-day Sir John Johnson, the 6th Baronet, writing in his 1963 book, *The North American Johnsons*, verified the rumor that Sir John invited Clarissa to come to Montreal. She did, and the two aging lovers had a quiet reunion. He gave her a house in Schenectady and an annuity of "one thousand pounds per annum." This is only partly true. According to Campbell's on-the-scene correspondence, he gave her a one-time gift of one thousand pounds, a certified letter authorizing a draft on him for the purchase of a house, and a pledge to honor an annual 50 pound per-year life annuity. He then wrote, "This arrangement will ease your mind and make your latter days more comfortable, as the idea of it does mine." The home was on the north side of State Street, the site of the present Schenectady Savings & Loan Association. Years later, she deeded this house over to her son-in-law James Van Horne, by then a prominent Schenectady merchant, after which it was generally known as Van Horne Hall. It burned in 1934.

Clarissa and John's daughter, Margaret Van Horne, bore four children but died while on a visit to Tribes Hill relations at a fairly youthful age. Their son William married a Canadian girl, Margaret Clark, with whom he had five children, one of whom he named Clarissa Ann. Through his father's connections, he obtained the position of Overseer of the Locks at Cascades, Ontario. He died in 1836 aged 66.

In mid July 1815, Lady Polly Watts Johnson became seriously ill. She remained so for three weeks and died on the 7th of August, aged 61. Sir John had 15 more years to live, Clarissa 18. Their long-time go-between, Daniel Campbell, had already died in 1802. To what extent they corresponded directly thereafter is unknown, but some correspondence probably ensued.

Clarissa lived in Schenectady the rest of her life. She is easily discovered in the U.S. Censuses of 1790 through 1830. In 1790 she is listed under her real first name Cornelia, as having a household that included one slave. In the 1810 and 20 censuses, she is listed as Clara. She died, aged 82 on July 1st, 1833 and is buried in the large Van Horne lot at Vale Cemetery.

In the ensuing years after Colonel Briggs retired from Johnson Hall and Mrs. Wanda Burch took over, the modern-day Clarissa referred to in the first paragraph of this essay returned to Johnson Hall several times. The last time she visited, it was on an occasion when the staff was particularly busy. No one had a chance to ask her where she lived or about her genealogy. She has not returned since.

Historian John Vrooman wrote his book about Clarissa with no knowledge of the Johnson-Putman-Campbell correspondence located in a library not far from his home. In the late 1940's, when the lettering on Clarissa Putman's grave stone was still legible someone thought enough to record her hand-cut epitaph. It reads, "Here to the dreary grave confined, she sleeps in death's dark gloom. Until the eternal morning wakes, the slumber of the tomb."

As far as posterity goes, Clarissa Putman in one way has been more fortunate than Sir John. Her Vale Cemetery, grave in the Van Horne lot is well maintained, whereas Sir John Johnson's family crypt containing his remains, those of Lady Polly and several of their children, was bulldozed into a ravine in 1950 by an historically-unimpressed land-owner. Archaeologists are still sorting the bones.

Clarissa Putman's ancestors and those of many other Dutch families, predated the English take-over of New Netherlands. They adapted to life under English colonial government, paid it lip-service, profited from it, and when English rule self-destructed, the Dutch remained.

Peter Betz is a retired librarian from Fulton-Montgomery Community College in Johnstown, New York. He currently serves as a councilman in the Town of Perth and is the official historian for Fulton County. The above essay was presented as a talk at Old Fort Johnson, just a couple of weeks before the destructive flood from Tropical Storm Irene swept through the first floor of that historic structure.

Not Either/Or

by Mary Clemens

It happened this morning at eight-thirty. I sat down and said to myself, "What am I doing and why am I doing it?" Up since four, stock fed, firewood stacked and ready for the day, stalls cleaned and muck moved to where it ought to be, I finished rebuilding the fire in my woodstove and wondered at my life. How did this happen?

This isn't the first time I've wondered. A single woman who buys her first horse farm in her fifth decade should expect to be surprised. Instead of sublime peace and quiet there are near neighbors who celebrate everything with fireworks. It's a sad revelation that the FBI statistics (so earnestly consulted pre-purchase) don't cover country crimes like a sneak's midnight raid on the paddock. Of course, there are the biting dogs who roam when they should stay home. And those coyote howls that somehow enter the blood through the ear, an impossible and primitive feat that keeps me awake until I get up to do it all over again.

So why did I do it: leave a life of pretty cushy comfort in a suburban condo? And why do I do it still, especially as I age in a world that thinks all age craves is comfort?

Here's why: it is dark night, even though I've already risen and gone to feed the horses The moon is such a brilliant white disc I can discard the flashlight and still find my way. I'm alone, except for the occasional shift worker passing in his car, and, of course, except for the horses. They stand in the deepest part of the shed but still the wind rakes their manes.

That wind numbs not just my flesh but my mind (farm work is often routine for a reason). But, despite the cold, despite the wind, despite the dark and early hour -- or because of them -- there is fresh joy to be had here and now. It's not a discrete joy (the package you unwrap at Christmas or the egg your child finds at the Easter hunt). It's a slow, quiet, insidious, comprehensive and most surprising joy and it emerges from this unlikeliest place, time and temperature.

And that's why I do it.

I moved to the Mohawk valley for predictable, practical reasons: it's great land for grazing; it's cheaper to keep the horses home than to board them; it's a beautiful setting for a writer who needs inspiration. But I stayed because it's a far more complete experience than you get where I come from. Here, joy springs from existence not from occasion.

You can't avoid things here as you can in the city where the anonymous or branded supply life's (not always) necessities as you recede through a series of closing doors until, behind your own, you are finally closed off completely. There, so many joys seem prefabricated, a product off the shelf, something to consume. And, where I come from, it's an either/or existence. You can pretty much structure your life to be comfortable or you can't and then, except perhaps for family and God, there's astonishingly little comfort to be had. You have or you have not.

But here in the valley everything combines: you may be impoverished but rich in land; your roof leaks but the view from your window is magnificent. You work too hard but the work is good work to do, essential, in fact, and doesn't require anything that makes it hard for you to sleep at night. That's real joy, to me. To me, that's worth something.

Someone once said "the man who fears death also fears life." Here, death is an everyday thing not a headline-grabber. The bird baby who falls too early from the nest, the rabbit caught by a cat, the logger felled by a tree: their passings are mixed up with life so thoroughly that they become normal. Sorrow says good-bye to dread and truly, deeply, harshly, gorgeously life goes on.

This summer, in the valley, tornadoes and floods proved that truth. Severed bridges, lost land and lost life, shock, hard work, avoidance, epiphany abducted the summer that should have been devoted to cultivation. For many it was a total loss.

With reflection, the mad weather seems almost biblical but, in the moment, it was as grotesque and hurtful and meaningless as a surgeon's mistake, the amputation of the wrong hand. There are those who will recover and there are those who will feel the loss as a phantom limb, who will make pain out of nothingness because even pain is better than nothing when there is truly nothing left.

We think we make choices: to walk out into the moonlight silting to earth or to sleep; to love, to work, to marry and have kids -- or not. To live under the tiny thumb of man or the huge eye of God. But it's all part of the hash that surrounds us.

Tone-deaf or not, each day that we rise and go on with our tasks we also hum an existential little ditty. That's how and when it all comes together. Nowhere is that more true than in this valley where joy is real and so is loss and neither can be ignored so it's never either/or.

Mary Clemens is a former actor, student, teacher and psychotherapist but always a writer. She's glad she learns a lot from life.

The Broken Heart of Amsterdam

Bert Nepaulsingh, PhD

Amsterdam, this small city, has had its big, big heart broken many times. The changing beat of Amsterdam's big heart has been well documented, especially by historians like Washington Frothingham, Max Reid, Nelson Green, Hugh Donlon, Jackie Murphy, Kelly Yacobucci, Gerry Snyder, Bob Cudmore, Robert von Hasseln, and others. Thanks to the careful documentation of these historians, and with the visual aid of photographers like John Maney and Mark Perfetti, Amsterdam's capacity to renew itself seems more important and obvious than the damaging changes wrought upon the city. Not the decline of traffic on the Mohawk Turnpike, nor the decreasing number of packet boats on the Erie Canal, nor the disappearance of the mills, nor the major errors of Urban Renewal--not one of the turbulent upheavals in the history of the city has diminished the potential of Amsterdam to shape an exciting future.

Amsterdam's future should always include wise ways to incorporate its past. And, whatever future is designed for Amsterdam, the section of the city that the Historic League of Amsterdam has called "The Heart of Amsterdam," should help shape visions for the future of the big-hearted little city. But the major problem with visions, obviously, is that no two pairs of eyes see exactly the same way. The vision of a newcomer, for example, cannot precisely be the same as the vision of a native. Most natives seem to have a unique genetic attachment to the place of their birth that newcomers cannot have. And yet, there is a real sense in which newcomers and natives might love the same place in different ways that yield the same positive results.

For example, a native born in Amsterdam in December of 1967, when the city's Common Council officially launched its program for Urban Renewal, will not have lived in Amsterdam's history as long as a newcomer who came to Amsterdam long before 1967 and has loved the city ever since. In fact, many natives know less about the place of their birth than newcomers who have taken the trouble to study a city's history and transport themselves into that city's past. In other words, both natives and newcomers who love a city like Amsterdam might do well to pose their visions for the city in the form of questions rather than as mandatory dogmatic solutions, politics and democratic elections notwithstanding.

Natives and newcomers who love Amsterdam should imagine positive reasons to look at the Mall, for example, and see, not failed Urban Renewal planning, but questions about the suitability of certain kinds of space. For example, approaching Exit 27 on I-90 West, does Amsterdam not appear, nestled on the banks of the Mohawk, like a beautiful surprise on a wooded landscape? Does Amsterdam not look, nestled there, young and fresh, like a sophisticated College Town, the kind of wise and learned space where town and gown embrace each other with mutual respect? Approaching Exit 27, traveling west, with the cruise control set at about 74 miles per hour to avoid the radar traps at Schenectady, Rotterdam, and elsewhere, is it not a brief and pleasant twenty minutes ago from Exit 24? And, is not Exit 24 on I-90 a place where the University at Albany is currently bursting at its seams with nanotechnology and other forms of new knowledge, as is equidistant Malta, by the way?

Looking at the Mall again, just twenty minutes from the University at Albany, does that mall not look now like ideal classroom space, complete with offices and staff and student parking lots? Instead of mourning and whining and wringing of the hands in anguish about the Mall, can the big-hearted little city not remind the University at Albany, in a carefully prepared presentation, about its long-standing connections with Amsterdam? Have not anthropologists and gerontologists and historians and social scientists at the University at Albany not done invaluable research in Amsterdam? Is there not a great deal more research in gerontology and history that can be done, at Amsterdam's Wilkinson Facility and Walter Elwood Museum, for example? Is there not incomparably cheap housing in Amsterdam for newcomer faculty and staff and students, only twenty minutes from Albany, as well as for natives of Amsterdam?

And if, by some silly chance, the University at Albany were to decline Amsterdam's well-reasoned presentation, is the Mall not useable as Community College space? While it is true that young and eager residents of Amsterdam now drive, not always easily, to Fulton Montgomery Community College, and Schenectady Community College, and even Hudson Valley Community College, is it not also true that the graduates of Amsterdam High deserve their own Amsterdam Community College? And, is there not a deserved emphasis, at the federal level, on educating a globally competitive workforce for the future economic well-being of the United States? And then, again, speaking of economic development and well-being, is Amsterdam, in terms of its historical importance, not as good and as under-exploited a tourist attraction, as any other place in the State of New York? In fact, is there any place in New York State, or in the United States, for that matter, with a better riverfront tourist potential than Amsterdam, New York, on the Erie Canal? The tours conducted and planned by the Historical League of Amsterdam are an excellent beginning, but can there not be a professionally planned international tourist package, one-day round trip from New York City, for example, around a theme something like "From Amsterdam of the Netherlands to New Amsterdam to Amsterdam New York"? Are there not several other ethnic groups, not just the Dutch, but also the Polish, the Italian, the Palatine German, the Puerto Rican, the Latin American, whose "roots" tourists now spend millions of dollars everyday in New York City, and who might be tempted by a one-day professionally promoted side trip to the small city with a big unbreakable heart?Every lot in what the Historical League correctly calls "The Heart of Amsterdam", bounded roughly by Lower Church Street, Greenhill Cemetery, and the Riverfront Mall, has a story most roots tourists would be delighted to pay money to hear.

For example, we know that the name Kellogg is a brand name throughout the United States; and we know, as well, that the Kelloggs who started the linseed oil business in West Galway are an important family, historically, to Amsterdam. Less well known is that the most successful member of the Amsterdam branch of the Kellogg family was Spencer Kellogg, the one who left his native Amsterdam to become a newcomer in other parts of western New York State. At the height of his commercial success, and at the request of his son, Donald, Spencer Kellogg paid to have printed and bound, privately in

1914, only 100 copies of a book he called *From Boyhood to Manhood*. Since Spencer Kellogg moved from his native West Galway to Amsterdam with his parents when he was only six months old, his book about his boyhood is an important primary source about the history of lots and parcels in The Heart of Amsterdam.

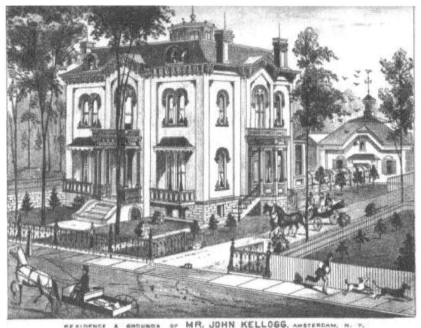

RESIDENCE & GROUNDS OF MR. JOHN KELLOGG, AMSTERDAM, N. Y.

The title of Spencer Kellogg's book is explained by his statement that "it is a mystery how so many boys live to manhood" (143). He and his cousin George and their friends were involved in so many dangerous teenage hijinks that Spencer marveled, as he wrote his memoirs for his children, how he managed to survive to manhood and be a father. For example, when Spencer was eighteen years old in 1869, the Second Presbyterian Church at the corner of Grove and Church Streets was being rebuilt, and the workmen had placed an unseemly rag on a pole at the top of the steeple (173). Spencer and his friends were playing in the churchyard when one of them said that the rag on the pole was a disgrace to their church, and they decided that they would climb the workmen's scaffold and remove the rag and pole. Spencer said that he tried to dissuade his friends, but when they ignored him, he decided to climb with them. As they climbed farther and farther up the scaffolding, most of the boys "chickened out" and climbed down. Then, about five levels of scaffolding below the tip of the steeple, the ringleader of the pack of teenagers, the one Spencer had tried to dissuade, decided he would go no farther. Instead of following the ringleader down, Spencer became emboldened, having reached so high, that he decided to continue to the tip of the steeple on his own. When he reached the very tip, Spencer looked down to see that a crowd had gathered. He removed the rag and pole and threw it down to the crowd; then he took out his knife and carved his initials "S.K." on the globe that was below the cross at the steeple's tip (174).

Spencer's story is interesting for us today, not just because of his adventure, but especially because of the details he provides about lots, parcels, and houses in the Heart of Amsterdam. He wrote, for example, that his mother "who happened to be at the window of our house at the time (which was about one and a half blocks away) noticed the crowd and saw someone climbing the steeple, but did not think it was I, or, as she told me later, she would have been very much frightened" (175). With the help of maps and directories, we can locate the house to which Spencer is referring: the *Schenectady and Amsterdam Directory* for 1876-77 lists "Kellogg Elizabeth, widow Lorin, house 27 Church" (186). The fact that the Elizabeth Kellogg listed in this directory was Lauren Kellogg's widow also helps to provide us with ample details about the house on 27 Church Street, because Spencer Kellogg included a photograph of it in his memoir where he described it as the rented brick house on Church Street in which he "spent about eighteen years of [his] life" (58).

About the Second Presbyterian Church itself, Spencer Kellogg wrote that "the original. . . Church, corner of Church and Grove streets, was built in 1836" (171). This original church had no steeple, judging from the photograph provided by Kellogg facing page 162. The steeple Kellogg climbed was on the church completed in 1869, and Spencer made the interesting request that people "living when this steeple is pulled down [should] look for [his] initials", that is, the initials S.K. that he carved on the globe beneath the cross at the tip of the steeple. The church burned down in 2000 when it was

Second Presbyterian Church, Amsterdam, N. Y.

being renovated, and it would be worthwhile to find out if the globe on the steeple was examined for Kellogg's initials. Chances are, that since only 100 copies of Kellogg's memoirs were printed, few people knew of his request.

The architects who rebuilt the Second Presbyterian Church had the good aesthetic sense to retain a similar steeple in the new building, removing the cross at the very top, but keeping a globe beneath where the cross used to be. This architectural note is significant because, by contrast, the buildings on the west side of Church Street, diagonally across from the Presbyterian church, where the jail, and a residence, and a mill used to be, were replaced in 1974 by a jarring and aesthetically discordant structure which now houses Amsterdam's Fire Department, City Court, and Police Station. In other words, Amsterdam's big heart was broken one more time when this new structure was erected as an injustice to Amsterdam's architectural and historical past. What can be done about this injustice, except, perhaps, to make sure that the justice dispensed in the court and police station is not criminal? Are there photographs of the home, jail, and mill? Will the directories help identify what was lost, so that a professional tour guide could restore the loss in the imagination of future tourists? Can parcel histories and historical markers not be placed as tourist guides on every lot at which the big heart of Amsterdam was broken?

One ideal candidate for such a tourist historical marker would be the property that James A. Miller bought in 1863 from the heirs of Alexander Sheldon, according to Book 77, pages 328-329 of the Montgomery County Grantors and Grantees Index. This property, or a great portion of it, including the vacant lot called City Park, now belongs to City Hall. On that vacant lot, James A. Miller built a house of the same design as the house built by his business partner John Kellogg around 1858. James Miller and John Kellogg were both uncles of Spencer Kellogg, and Spencer provides valuable information about both his uncles in his memoir. For example, Spencer tells his readers exactly why Miller might have built the house on the property he bought from Alexander Sheldon's heirs.

"My Uncle Jim and Aunt Lizzie," Spencer wrote, "had a family of one boy and two girls, John, Katie, and Lizzie" (25). Little Lizzie died of scarlet fever when she was only five years old, and when her cousin Spencer was still a small child not much older than she; since Spencer was born in 1851, Lizzie must have died in the late 1850s. "Aunt Lizzie," Spencer explained, "was prostrated with grief. She would not be comforted, would spend hours crying over the little playthings which belonged to her little daughter. Uncle Jim tried to divert her mind, but with little success, and I remember hearing our people say that they thought she would lose her mind. Uncle Jim purchased another house, thinking that by taking her out of and away from these environments she might not be reminded so much of Lizzie. This occurred about a year after her death. The house they moved into was a beautiful brick house opposite ours. They formerly lived on Grove Street, and we lived on Church Street. Even after they moved to this new house, Aunt would cry nights when alone" (27).

RESIDENCE & GROUNDS OF MR. JAMES A. MILLER, AMSTERDAM, N. Y.

Spencer's account means that little Lizzie died on Grove Street, and that to comfort her mother and namesake, James Miller bought a house on the west side of Church Street, opposite 27 Church Street on the east side, where Spencer and his mother lived in a rented house. But since Elizabeth Miller was not sufficiently comforted even in the new house, James must have decided to try to comfort his wife by building a larger more elaborate structure on the huge parcel of land he bought from the Sheldon estate in 1863. Since the large house Miller built has now disappeared, there is much confusion about

James A. Miller

where it existed. To clear up as much of the confusion about the Miller House, here are some facts.

James A. Miller was born in Glasgow, Scotland, June 30, 1821; he died in Amsterdam, December 27, 1904. Miller had been brought to New York, at age nine, where he had started work as a clerk in NYC at age sixteen. Miller spent time in Galway where his parents owned a farm. Moving to Fultonville, Miller made quite a fortune saving and investing, while working for steamboat owner, John Starin. In 1836, Miller married Elizabeth Clark from Galway (and Massachusetts), not Elizabeth Kellogg. Because there was an Elizabeth Kellogg, it has been incorrectly stated that James Miller was John Kellogg's brother-in-law. Lauren Kellogg, John's brother, married Elizabeth Miller, James Miller's sister. James Miller was Lauren Kellogg's brother-in-law.

KELLOGG & MILLER'S LINSEED OIL WORKS, AMSTERDAM, N. Y.

With his money, Miller invested in the Kellogg Linseed Oil company, apparently as a senior partner; apparently senior, because the parcel of land he bought on Church Street next to his partner Kellogg's lot was much much larger than the lot numbered 47 which Kellogg bought, by the way, from John and Elizabeth McClumpha, as explained below.

A map in the rare 1868 *Atlas of Montgomery and Fulton Counties* makes it quite clear that the Miller House is due north of the Kellogg House, that is, up from Kellogg toward Sanford/ City Hall. Nevertheless, some people believe that the houses are reversed, with the Kellogg house north and having disappeared, and the Miller house as having survived. Several authoritative documents, including the Manuals of the Board of Trade and the Directories, indicate without reason for doubt that traveling north, Kellogg's House comes before Miller's.

James Miller Carriage House, 2011. Photo by Victor Grant.

Whereas Kellogg's lot was always 47, Miller owned the carriage house behind the Kellogg house. Miller's carriage house appears in the Amsterdam Directories as 51, not 49, after Kellogg's 47. In other words, the lot was double, at least, and the carriage house accounts for the missing number 49 in the directories. Although he owned it outright, Miller shared that carriage house with the Kelloggs, and, according to the book of deeds (169, page 315 and 585, page 115) there is still an easement today, apparently, from the Kellogg house to the carriage house, and for about nine feet from High street to the carriage house.

The Amsterdam Directories also show no numbers from Miller's house, 51, to what is now City Hall, which is number 61. For accuracy, a surveyor should mark off the distances in the deeds, but by rough estimate, the estate Miller bought from Alexander Sheldon on August 25, 1863, for $7600, was more than one acre and one rood large, much larger, that is, than the lot John Kellogg had bought from John and Elizabeth McClumpha on April 2, 1855. Miller's property, and/or his neighbor's, seems to reach into Green Hill cemetery, where there was/is a memorial to soldiers maintained by the Grand

Army of the Republic. This is probably why some of my PAV neighbors have told me that they were directed to the Daughters of the American Republic for use of the park. The DAR probably shared responsibilities with the GAR.

On a map dated 1853, there is clearly a structure on the lot next to what later became the Sanford Mansion. This, no doubt, not the Miller house, is the structure Amsterdam City Historian Robert von Hasseln refers to as having been acquired by Sanford in 1895 and razed (*Heart of Amsterdam*, page 15).

When Miller died in 1904, his wife Elizabeth (Clark) Miller inherited his estate, including the Miller house. And when Elizabeth Miller died, her daughter Catherine (Miller) Holbrook inherited the Miller estate. After Catherine Holbrook died, her brother, John Holbrook, sold the Miller estate, including the Miller house, to John Sanford, son of Stephen Sanford, on March 10, 1913 (*Montgomery County Deed Book* 154, pages 326-328, Book 164, pages 378-380, Book 173, pages 335-338).

In the *Amsterdam Directory* for 1913-14, the Miller house is listed as "vacant", because Catherine Miller had died. From 1913 or 1914, John Sanford used the Miller House for his employees, first for E. P.Truett (1914 to 1916 or 1917); then for William Ross (around 1917 to 1922); and then for William H. Paton, "General Superintendent at Sanford and Son" (1922 to around 1924).

By 1925, William Paton had died, and his widow, Clara, is listed as living in the Miller House. Suddenly, the Directory "beginning October 1927" lists Clara Paton as having moved to 25 Market Street, and more significantly, the same directory lists no building on the lot numbered 51 Church Street. This seems to mean that the Miller house was razed sometime between 1925 and before October 1927.

A neighbor has told me that he read somewhere that the Miller House burned down, and that there was suspicion about the fire; that an investigation was conducted that might have ruled out arson but that excavated the foundations of the Miller house. I have good reason to believe this neighbor, especially because, Catherine Holbrook's husband, George M. Holbrook was an insurance agent with an office at 56 East Main Street.

There might have been rumors, true or false, that the house was torched for insurance money.

I feel confident about resolving the fire theory sometime soon, either with the book my neighbor read somewhere, or with the help of fire reports, including those in local newspapers.

Since 1932, when John Sanford gave the Miller estate to City Hall, the Miller estate has been named as part of City Hall Park. One wonders who owns and maintains the carriage house, which should not be demolished but restored for the sake of history, as the Kellogg and Miller Carriage House.

A similar parcel history as attempted here for the Miller property can be written for all the absent lots and parcels within the rough boundary of the Riverfront Mall, Church Street, and the Green Hill Cemetery. The result of these parcel histories could be a worthwhile *History of the Big Unbreakable Heart of Amsterdam*.

Bert Nepaulsingh is a professor of Latino and Caribbean Studies at the University of Albany and lives in the former Kellogg House in Amsterdam.

Montgomery County's Okwari Park Fiasco

Daniel T. Weaver

The Montgomery Board of Supervisors dreamed big back in the late 60s and early 70s. They dreamed of an all season 3,673 acre park that would have two man-made lakes and a large pond, trailer and tent sites, cabins, a motel and conference center, riding stables, two marinas, two beach facilities, a conservation education center, a model farm, cross country, hiking and riding trails, two swimming pools, a hunting preserve, an amphitheater and a nine hole golf course with room to expand to eighteen.

In February 1973, Saratoga Associates released it's 138 page comprehensive plan for the proposed Okwari Park. The plan did not leave out a single detail, including a full color map of the proposed park. The park would lie in the towns of Charleston and Root, with its southern boundary abutting the town of Carlisle in Schoharie County. Okwari is the Mohawk word for bear, and the site of the park was traditionally known as Bear Swamp.

There were several reasons why the Board of Supervisors wanted the park. First, there was no large publicly developed recreational site in the the county at the time. Secondly, because there were limited recreational facilities in the county, 63% of county residents left the county on Sundays for recreation in other nearby counties. Thirdly, the size and diverse opportunity for recreation in Okwari Park would not only keep residents in the county but would draw people from outside the county. Fourthly, the park would provide opportunity for employment and potential for revenue and land development near the park.

The cost-benefit analysis by Saratoga Associates included four possible scenarios.

1. That the park would provide no financial benefits to Montgomery County, and there would be no benefits from adjacent land development. Saratoga Associates saw this as an extremely improbable outcome.

2. That there would be benefits from the park but no benefits from adjacent land development. This scenario would be only remotely possible, according to Saratoga Associates.

3. The park would provide benefits and moderate benefits from adjacent land development. It was the park planners' judgment that this was the most likely scenario.

4. The park would provide benefits plus rapid adjacent land development benefits. The planners stated that this was possible, but did not state that it was probable.

In order to spread out costs, the plan was to build the park in stages with land acquisition beginning in 1972; the upper lake, golf course and ski area construction beginning in 1973, etc. until the final phase of building which would end in 1978. There is little doubt that Okwari Park was going to be a beautiful park. But Okwari Park never got beyond the comprehensive master plan and the acquisition of land.

Two headlines below the fold of the *Amsterdam Recorder* on November 7, 1973 said, "Nixon Secretary to Testify at Missing Tape Hearing" and "Nixon on TV Tonight." The top headline above the fold was "County Voters KO Bond Issue, Okwari." KO was the right word as voters turned down Local Proposition One—Should Montgomery County complete the entire Okwari Park project?—by a vote of 14,736-1,583. Voters defeated Local Proposition Two—Should Montgomery County complete only phase one of the Okwari Park project?—by a vote of 13,641-1,940. Even the voters in the Towns of Charleston and Root, where the park site was located, voted against the park, although the vote was closer.

It would appear that the voters did not accept Saratoga Associates' scenario #3 above; rather they thought that scenario #1 would have been the likely outcome of building the park.

But even if the voters had not rejected the park, it is unlikely it could have been built. Just a few days before the referendum, the New York State Department of Environmental Conservation refused to grant Montgomery County permission to build a series of dams on Fly and Flat creeks, dams necessary for building the two lakes in the park. The county would have had to take EnCon to court in order to get the decision overturned. A lawsuit would have been iffy to start with, but with the people's rejection of the park, it was pointless.

The county needed to acquire 75 parcels of land, either by purchase or eminent domain, in order to build the park. The acquisition process itself became controversial with the supervisors complaining about the property appraisal process in a September 1972 meeting that did not allow them to approve of purchase agreements. After the election, the county was left with 800 acres of land to dispose of. The Board of Supervisors voted to give the original property owners first chance to buy their land back. It was a lame duck Board of Supervisors who initially dealt with undoing what had been already done in anticipation of the park because the voters not only defeated the Okwari Park proposition, they voted out of office almost every supervisor who supported the park.

The Republican Party benefited from the vote. Following the elections, the Board of Supervisors' make-up changed from an even mix of Democrats and Republicans to eleven Republicans, six Democrats and one Independent. Six incumbent supervisors were defeated, and the new board had ten new supervisors altogether. The Board of Aldermen in Amsterdam went from six Democrats and two Republicans to four Republicans, three Democrats and third ward Alderman, Raymond Hall, although a Democrat, ran as a Conservative, Independent, and Liberal.

Opposition to the park had been voiced loudly, even before the election. Candidates who were running against incumbents, capitalized on the opposition. A campaign ad in the *Amsterdam Recorder* for Bill Johnson running for 8th Ward Supervisor in the City of Amsterdam stated:

"Let's look at the Official Voting Record of the Present 8th Ward Supervisor [John Bien]. Between 4/12/66 and 12/30/72 He Voted On 28 Resolutions Regarding Okwari Park. For Okwari Park – 25 times. Against Okwari Park – 3 times."

Incumbent aldermen in the City of Amsterdam, while having no official say in county matters, used the Okwari Park issue to help get themselves re-elected. A campaign ad to Re-Elect Joseph M. Purtell, Alderman of the 8th Ward, which appeared in the *Amsterdam Recorder* on November 2, 1973, said that Purtell had "Demanded a full accounting, tax cost of Okwari Park to 8th Ward Residents and demanded by resolution to stop all further expenditure." The 8th ward re-elected Purtell.

Controversy over the park had reached such a state in January of 1973, that the following letter was published in the *Amsterdam Recorder*.

"Dear Editor: There has recently been much public comment on Montgomery County's Okwari Park project with the latest coming from what is apparently a publicity seeking source...We need no high pressure public relations effort to guide us as to our responsibilities...As to the Okwari Park Project, it should be noted that this project was started in 1966 and has been closely watched, guided and our people's interest protected in every stage of its development. We continue our effort here and mean to see that good "value" and benefit comes not only to the county as a whole but that the people of the city of Amsterdam are well represented and will be pleased with the results."

The letter, dated January 15, 1973, was signed by all eight Amsterdam supervisors which included: Marcus Breier, First Ward; Thomas McNamara, Second Ward; Chester Iwanski, Third Ward; Ambrose Krupcsak, Fourth Ward; Louis Sandy, Fifth Ward; Anthony Barone, Sixth Ward; Raymond Dybas, Seventh Ward and John Bien, Eighth Ward.

Whether or not Okwari Park should have been built is debatable. What is not debatable is that it was a political boondoggle. The project was doomed when politicians and planners did not get the people's permission before beginning the project, nor the state's permission to build dams. The project wasted a lot of time and money. One million dollars had already been borrowed. $600,000 had already been spent on the project, some of which would be recouped when acquired property had been sold.

The real tragedy of Okwari Park, was not that the park was defeated by the voters, but rather, as a *Recorder* editorial stated, it might have been because the voters' rejected several experienced and effective supervisors who supported the park.

Observing The Passing Of Summer 2011 In Upstate New York

L. D. Davidson

---In the back field a turkey hen is marching with five turkey chicks toward the woods…

---For more than forty years now Edmund Wilson, the American literary critic, has not traveled to his summer home at Talcottville…

---A man at the Thursday evening chess club complains about paying $8,000 in property and school taxes on a property valued at $350,000. In North Carolina, he claims, he would be paying only $3,000.

---Perfectly honorable men wary of contact with women for fear that their motives will be incorrectly perceived…

---Union College's new supercomputer, donated by I.B.M. executive, an old alumnus of Union, who is quickly named the Vice Chairman of Union's Board of Trustees.

---Big fuss about the federal budget deficit. Obama caves to Tea party anti-tax partisans.

---At the summer concerts of the Philadelphia Orchestra at Saratoga, fireworks and light spectacles to market classical music…

---Bloated girls and women with romantic fantasies talking about being "looked at" by "creepers"…

---A great year for those who run major corporations or who want to use their wealth in order to influence elections or keep taxes low by protecting loopholes…no movement toward serious campaign finance reform…

---A lone coyote loping across the back field…

---To allow hydro-fracking or not to allow hydro-fracking? Fresh water shortage predicted by 2100. Governor Cuomo running for President in 2016…Business interests prevail—no surprise…

---At the Saratoga race track, cotton candy and junk food. The State Racing Commission paying their executives $400,000 per year while taking 20% of every dollar bet---still with a deficit of twenty million dollars…

---People so nationalistic in their myopic American orientation that they don't even have concept of what nationalism is…

---The baby boom generation (1945-1956) is entering retirement. Alzheimer Disease looms as a major health problem with financial consequences for the health care system. But no move from any source to expanding funding for treatment and cure…

---Lines for entry into the theatres for the last of the Harry Potter movies…

---Aging, tattooed NASCAR fans with pony-tails, fifty pounds overweight…

---The Obama Administration appoints two ex-banking executives, who soon will probably be future banking industry executives again, to be the key figures in shaping the new Consumer Protection Agency…

---The Yankees and the Red Sox vying for first place with their purchased and over paid stars. Are Alex Rodriegez and David Ortiz on a steroid program this season?

---Japanese beetles feasting on grapevines and plum leaves…

---Property taxes capped at 2%, but not really, and a weak plan to reform N.Y.S. government, but not really…

---A public librarian who organizes day care parties for toddlers and little children in library reading rooms, serving cookies and cupcakes to already overfed children, while turning away adult patrons who want to use the library for reading and study...

---The unemployment rate at 9.4% while multi-millionaire NBA players and owners squabble over dividing billions in revenues...

---A major flood of the Mohawk River and Schoharie Creek wrecks homes, bridges, farms and roads...Disaster relief is necessary...

---Standard and Poors, the financial rating agency, even with the aid of computers, or perhaps because of computers, makes a $2 trillion dollar calculation error leading to a downgrade of the credit rating of the U.S. government...

---Serial fund raising at the WMHT-FM, the classical radio station. Fund raising less for the sake of the classical music... rather classical music in short snippets for the purpose of fund raising...

---People so mentally dazed by commercial T.V. pseudo-reality that they no longer possess a concept of what "mediocrity" is...

---WAMC continuing their excellent public service programming. Alan Chartok seventy years old going on fifty...

---The Beech Nut operation completes its abandonment of Canajoharie, fled to a new plant facility twenty miles away in the Town of Florida...

---Furtive embraces and affectionate kisses, sheets dry and straight, one leg draped over another, moist heat of summer...

---Hamilton College finally succeeds in becoming a virtual country club for 18-22 year olds with club membership at more than $50,000 per year...but offering discounts called "scholarships" and "loans"...Classes offered for about 165 days per year...

---The first issue of *Upstream* magazine, a magazine of culture and history without any advertising...a new online newspaper begins publication, *The Mohawk Valley Independent*...

---Gloversville's Jewish Community Center building up for sale...not enough members left in that once thriving upstate community to sustain services...

---Volunteer fire departments perform great service helping flood victims...

---More than ten thousand runners compete in the Utica Boilermaker 15K road race...African runners in the top eight places...

---Bears moving into areas where they haven't been seen for one hundred years...

---Reductions in the budgets of schools and community organizations. Governor Andrew Cuomo against raising taxes for millionaires to raise more revenue for State coffers...

---A tornado touches down in Cranesville...

---Baseball tourism as usual at Cooperstown...

---And the insect world drones on oblivious to the concerns of mankind...

L. D. Davidson is a graduate of Harvard, a high school Latin teacher, a regular contributor to the *Sunday Gazette* (Schenectady, NY) and an orchardist specializing in heirloom apples.

Fundamentalism To Feminism - A Journey. Part Two

Ruth Peterson

Part I of this essay concluded, "Like the blazing sun, it had the warmth to begin a thaw in my frozen soul." I spoke of those brave, bold women who articulated what I knew to be true. The other "gospel truths" had been conveyed to me, not by some fly-by-night Elmer Gantry, but by "men of God," who were assured, charismatic and outwardly scholarly. As I began to doubt their creed, I began to believe some of the true life stories of women. I even dared to silently call myself a feminist, just one of those of either gender who believe in equality for all.

Feminism is a perfectly good word, but it has become tainted with images of women breaking down doors, using strident language, burning bras and resisting men whom they might formerly have loved and admired. Throughout my long life, I have loved men in my roles as daughter, wife, sister, mother, partner, friend, but I didn't quite fall into the camp of Friedan, Abzug, Steinem or Fonda.

Gender inequality became increasingly obvious to me while raising my family. I was living the gender roles of prior generations but I was constantly questioning them. As a tired housewife, I began to note the predominate gender of those in the corridors of power – in government, the professions, in science, in corporate board rooms, in the creative arts.

I pondered Tillie Olsen's book, *Silences*, in which she talks about why women have such long silences in their lives. They are bearing and bringing up children and advancing the careers of men.

I discovered that life's journey need not fossilize or freeze; it can be fluid, as we gradually catch glimpses of a better way of living and thinking. We need not deplore our former selves or our forebears, but may choose to look back with kindness and understanding and forward with optimism.

I was too busy then to drop everything – the baby, the toddler, the beds, the stove, the washing machine, the vacuum cleaner and the iron, but I began to realize why so many older women in my family became "in-valids" at mid-life. Many were hampered by strong religious beliefs and gender expectations.

Women were living longer, their children grew up and left. They excelled at the household arts, but were often ill-prepared to join those who wrote books, painted pictures, healed the sick, practiced law, performed music, climbed the corporate ladder, (forgetting or minimizing women's greatest contribution to society.)

I also began to see how religion has served as an approved strategy to lend power to men and to deprive women of many of the freedoms available to men. They were invoking "God," as the only infallible and just arbiter of the doings of humanity. Many societies throughout history have enthroned man as the head of woman; woman is a subsidiary who benefits from the largess of the powerful and "infallible" male.

In 1949, Simone de Beauvoir in *The Second Sex*, quotes the words of Aristotle, "The female is a female by virtue of a certain lack of qualities," (again overlooking her unique ability to reproduce). And St. Thomas pronounced woman to be an "imperfect man," an incidental being. De Beauvoir also sees this illustrated in Genesis where Eve is depicted as made from what theologian Jacque Bossuet in the 1600's called "a supernumerary," or extra bone of Adam.

Annie Gaylor Taylor has edited a book, *Women Without Superstition, - No Gods – No Masters*, compiling the writings of "Women Free Thinkers of the 19th and 20th Centuries." Long before Steinam, Abzug, Friedan or Fonda, women were making note of inequality.

In 1840, Elizabeth Stanton went with her husband to the World Anti-slavery Convention in London. The men voted, on the basis of scriptural edicts, to exclude women from participating, delegating them to a curtained-off area. Women, of course, had no vote. She writes that this marked the time when her feminist awareness was fully awakened.

Matilda Joslyn Gage, author dedicated to freeing women from the teachings of the Christian church, wrote, "the real foundation of the church is the doctrine of women's inferiority by reason of her "original sin.'" Helen H. Gardner wrote in her 1885 book, *Men, Women and God* - "This religion and the Bible require of woman everything and give her nothing. They ask her support and her love, and repay her with contempt and oppression."

Barbara Ehrenreich, well-known essayist, novelist, socialist and feminist of our day, is widely published in leading American journals, magazines and newspapers. In a 1981 essay, "U.S. Patriots: Without God on Their Side," she warned, "The threat we now face is as much political as it is in any spiritual sense, 'religious'...Christian revivalism has...passed itself off as the quintessential expression of Americanism...this mixture of religion and politics (branded 'theopolitics')...is a period when the male-dominated Christian Right...actually held state power...and when Sen. Joe McCarthy...declared that 'the fate of the world rests with the clash between the atheism of Moscow and the Christian spirit in other parts of the world.' It is at our peril that we underestimate the power of the 'radical right.'" And this fragment from contemporary Marge Piercy's poem entitled, "Right to Life," "Priests and Legislators do not hold/ shares in my womb or my mind./ This is my body. If I give it to you/ I want it back. My life/ Is a non-negotiable demand."

What I believe about men, women and religion does not lend itself neatly to categories – atheist, agnostic, "lapsed" Baptist, Reformed, Methodist or Unitarian. I would prefer to call myself a "free-thinker," but I am not completely free of early influences. Sometimes I want to shout, "Your god is too small" and I must remind myself we are all affected by nature and nurture. The birth of a baby, the opening of a rose, the galaxies above or a Mozart sonata below - all astound me. So does a tornado, a plane crash, an earthquake, a disastrous flood or a terrorist attack. Fundamentalist "believers" label all of these things "God's Will."

Several readers have said they would look forward to Part II of this essay. One asked, "How did your marriage turn out? " It did not survive, as one might expect. There was a lot of pain for the entire family due to that failure. Let me conclude, however, by saying that I did live to love again.

Ruth Peterson was a public relations professional for many years and has written Op-Ed pieces for *The Sunday Gazette* since 1993. She considers her four sons and one daughter her greatest legacy.

The Pharmacist's Daughter

Linda C.Wisniewski

She was a shy little girl, but when she sang in church, Mary Anne Krupsak's coloratura voice came through loud and clear. She simply loved to sing, and her mother, an accomplished pianist and violinist, encouraged her. In the following interview, Amsterdam native and former Lieutenant Governor of New York Mary Anne Krupsak answers a few questions for *Upstream*.

Lt. Gov. Mary Ann Krupsak & Governor Hugh Carey. NYS Archives.

What were your dreams and ambitions as a little girl?

"When I was 12 years old, I sang at the first Mass of a distant cousin who was ordained a priest in Michigan. The church was big and beautiful and filled with people. I was so frightened but God was with me and I sang Ave Maria, Salve Regina and Panus Angelicus."

"I expected to work in the music world in some capacity. I know that the opportunities I had to sing gave me a chance to increase my self-esteem and helped me in life. I studied voice and majored in history at the University of Rochester, because of its connection with the Eastman School of Music and its fine academic reputation. I sang in the Eastman Chorus as an undergraduate and enjoyed performing in many concerts."

But as she got older, Krupsak was attracted to the idea of public service. She credits the influence of her father and her maternal grandfather, Michael Wytrwal, who was Montgomery County representative to FDR's National Recovery Administration.

"All funds expended for bridges, roads and public works projects as well as coalitions among employers, workers and government created by the NRA," she says, were under her grandfather's leadership. "He never held office but people sought him out to help them get jobs and for help with their problems." When she attended St. Stanislaus School on Cornell Street, little Mary Anne went to her grandparents' home just down the street for lunch everyday. There, she saw people coming by to ask for his help.

As a girl seeing her family "serve the community as pharmacists and my father as an elected Supervisor added a dimension of awareness of needs in the community that could only be met by government intervention." Ambrose Sr. was Chairman of the Board of Supervisors and advocated for the creation of Fulton-Montgomery Community College and Montgomery County Nursing Home (now privately owned and operated as River Ridge Living Center at 100 Sandy Drive in Amsterdam).

What did you like best about growing up in Amsterdam?

"There was never a distinction between my brother and myself. My parents who were equals as professionals in their business encouraged both of us children to develop our talents. College was always an expectation for both of us." (Her brother,

Ambrose Michael Krupczak, became a doctor and still resides in Amsterdam.)

"I was born in 1932 and remember the strong sense of community in the Reid Hill neighborhood." Her parents, Mamie and Ambrose Krupczak were pharmacists who owned a drug store on Hibbard Street. "Across the street was an Italian grocery and fruit market, and on another corner, a meat market owned by a Polish family." Although the Krupczaks were members of St. Stanislaus Church, they often attended Mass in Auriesville during the summer. "I have always loved the beauty of the Mohawk River, especially the bend in the River near Auriesville," she says.

Her childhood was Depression-era but also the beginning of economic recovery. "No one I knew was rich," Krupczak says, "but we seemed, with family members helping one another, to have enough. My parents' drugstore also had a soda fountain and my father made his own ice cream. During the summers, my brother and I worked at the soda fountain and I have memories of people lining up for blocks on warm summer evenings to have my father's ice cream. It was the Ben and Jerry's of the time."

Do you think growing up Polish American was an advantage or a disadvantage?

"I think it was an advantage. There is a quality of community life that many ethnic people experience and enjoy. I always felt at home in ethnic communities at festivals and in churches, especially in Polish American communities when I traveled to every corner of New York State as Lieutenant Governor. The people of Buffalo, where it was said there were more Polish people than in Warsaw, especially made me feel at home and I do believe the extraordinary support I received there had a lot to do with propelling my candidacy to success. Earlier, in my elections to the State Legislature, I received extraordinary support from the Polish-American community in Schenectady as well as overwhelmingly in Amsterdam. Three of my grandparents were born in Poland and I visited Poland in the 1970s with a group of educators and public officials. It was still the time of the Cold War with the Soviet Union, but there was a spirit of self-determination in Poland that you could feel. You could almost sense that someday they would be free again and they are."

Krupsak was honored to be one of the Polish American officeholders chosen by President Carter to represent America at the investiture of Pope John Paul II. She traveled to Rome with then Senator from Maine Edmund Muskie, now deceased, and then Maryland Congresswoman, now Senator Barbara Mikulski, with whom she remains friends.

Like many Polish Americans, her family name has changed its spelling. She was told "many years ago, it was much longer than Krupczak. My father thought spelling the name as it was usually pronounced by non-Poles would simplify his children's lives, so he had our names legally changed before we went off to college. I kept the new spelling, Krupsak, earning my law degree and being admitted to the bar with that spelling, as well as having a political career as Krupsak. My brother changed his name back to Krupczak in medical school because as he told me, he wanted to remain a Jr."

How long ago did you leave Amsterdam and why?

"When I married in 1969, I was a member of the Assembly of New York and my husband, Edwin Margolis, and I bought my brother's home in Canajoharie, which he needed to sell so that he and his family could move to Syracuse. He was beginning a medical residency, and my sister-in-law was beginning legal studies at Syracuse Law School. In the 1980s, my husband became a Judge of the Court of Claims in Albany, and I was practicing law in New York City and Albany. We moved to Columbia County which was more convenient for travel between the two cities." Margolis died in 1993, but Krupczak still has relatives in Amsterdam and visits the city frequently.

"I always loved Amsterdam," she says, "and grieve for the loss of industry, the movement of so many businesses up Route 30 and away from the City and the changes those trends have brought to the residents because of the loss of an important tax base." She says she will "try to prevail on the new

Administration in Albany to be more pro-active in helping Amsterdam. I recently had an occasion to visit with Lieutenant Governor Robert Duffy and discussed Amsterdam's needs."

When did you first become involved in politics?

Krupsak worked for Governor Averell Harriman and then for Congressman Samuel Stratton before resigning to attend the University of Chicago. She also served as assistant counsel in the New York State Senate and then assistant counsel to the Speaker of the Assembly until her election to the State Assembly.

"I was elected to the Assembly in 1968 and served two terms there. After my district was dissolved in re-apportionment, I served one term in the New York State Senate."

As State Senator, Krupsak sponsored women's rights legislation and introduced a resolution proclaiming February 15, 1974 Susan B. Anthony Day.

In 1974, she says, she decided to seek the office of Lieutenant Governor. "It was the first time in a century that New York had an open primary for statewide offices and every office was open and available in a direct primary. Hugh Carey, a Congressman from Brooklyn, chose to run for Governor against the Democratic Party's Convention-selected candidate. I chose to run for Lieutenant Governor though I was not selected at the Democratic Party Convention." Both won, making Krupsak the first woman Lieutenant Governor in the country.

In 1976, Carey appointed her to the Commission on Management and Productivity in the Public Sector. Krupsak served as honorary chairperson of the "Committee of 51.3%" of women leaders who assisted in Jimmy Carter's Presidential campaign. Krupsak also participated in the 1977 International Women's Year Tribute in Houston.

During her term as Lieutenant Governor, Krupsak assumed an ombudsman role, traveling throughout New York to learn about issues concerning New York's residents and offer solutions.

What was it like to be involved in the women's movement? Were there any advantages or disadvantages to being a woman in politics?

"My election in 1974 coincided with the height of excitement brewing in the women's movement about equality of opportunity for women in all walks of life. The litany of injustice is well known: the glass ceiling in all occupations, unequal pay for equal work, unequal property and marriage laws and many others. My candidacy caught fire, and people gravitated to me in the ferment that was developing. I was the most qualified of the three candidates running in the Democratic primary, but Democratic Party leaders were panicked that if I won I might pull our candidate down to defeat. Prejudice against women in politics was alive and well as in most fields. My party offered me impossible options: a chance to run against Jacob Javits, a popular incumbent United States Senator, or for Attorney General or anything else so that I would not be linked in the general election with the gubernatorial candidate and in their opinions bring the party to defeat. I refused. After the general election, when polls were conducted, it was found that my candidacy, rather than being an obstacle, actually brought two percent more votes to our ticket!"

What do you think was accomplished by the women's movement?

"I have never regretted any fight I was involved in, from bringing to creation laws to protect women and children from domestic violence, to better and more educational opportunities so that society benefits from the best of our people and not just one gender." Speaking of the Women's Movement, she remarked, "We were few in number and always had to prove ourselves."

The New York State Commissioner of Education at the time was quoted as saying that true equality would come "when women schlemiels could succeed equally with male schlemiels. The point is most women in public arenas had to be perceived as exceptional or having more credentials than a man seeking the same position." Krupczak was part of the Second Wave of feminism, the first being the suffragists who worked for women's right to vote. She knew and worked with Bella Abzug and Gloria Steinem, who helped her become known in New York City.

In 1978, Krupsak ran against Carey for the Democratic nomination for governor of New York. "Many people did not understand why I did that," she says. "It was largely my impatience with the pace of state government addressing chronic economic problems upstate." Carey gave her several high-profile assignments, including one to Washington to lobby the Texas delegation for federal aid to New York City. She wasn't sure she could do it, but Carey told her, "You can handle it. I know you can."

Did you meet any of the famous feminist leaders of the 70s?

Women leaders like Bella Abzug and Betty Friedan helped her with fundraising, Krupsak said, but "I came from such a small city (Amsterdam) no one thought my base was large enough to win" the nomination.

Krupsak and Steinem still connect through the Matilda Joslyn Gage Foundation, where Krupsak serves on the Board and Steinem on the National Advisory Council. Gage was a 19th century suffrage leader whose role was never fully appreciated or understood. In the past seven years, the Foundation has restored her home outside Syracuse and are helping to bring her works to the general public. "Her ideas and thoughts, especially about the slave trade in women and children, are as pertinent today as they were in the 19th century," Krupsak said.

When she moved to the Finger Lakes after her husband's death in 1993, Seneca Falls community leaders asked her to chair a committee to celebrate the 150th anniversary of the First Women's Rights Convention, held there in 1848.

During this period, Krupsak met Sally Roesch Wagner, a leading women's studies scholar who told her about Gage. An interesting fact she discovered is that "Frank Baum, creator of the Wizard of Oz books, was Gage's son-in-law and Gage encouraged him to write his stories with their many meanings, including the strength of women and the importance of peace." Krupsak incorporated a not-for-profit corporation for the Gage Foundation and is a volunteer legal adviser in addition to her role as Board member.

What would you say to a woman interested in entering public life today?

"Political campaigns have always cost too much, and it has always been especially hard for women. For the most part, we are idealists who want to serve to help make things better and too often contributions are made with expectations of access for personal gain." Still, she encourages women to choose public service because it "is personally rewarding and fulfilling to see good come to others through our work."

She is often sought out by women candidates and tries to advise and help as much as she can. She was an investor in three restaurants in the Finger Lakes in recent years and held an event at one of them for Kirsten Gillibrand, New York's junior senator, shortly after Gillibrand took office.

What is your life like today?

"I live on the east side of Seneca Lake and enjoy the beautiful sunsets." She is retired from law practice but is active in Our Lady of Peace Parish in Geneva and continues to support St. Stanislaus parish in Amsterdam financially. A few years ago, she spoke at a fundraising dinner to save St. Stanislaus School, "which I attended through eighth grade. I was sorry to see it close. The issues I care about are education of our young, entitlement programs for the needy and elderly and environmental challenges that may threaten the purity of the Finger Lakes. I contribute to local candidates and state and national candidates I feel are going to work for the values I believe in."

What would you like to be your legacy?

"To the extent I have a legacy, I hope it would be that I worked hard and honestly to make life better for people. I did not work exclusively on women's issues although I led on many. I worked for economic improvement all over our state and had some successes. When grape farmers upstate asked for my help in finding markets to replace the loss of sales for Welch's grape juice, my investigations uncovered obstacles to wine making and we made changes. Today we have a burgeoning wine industry that attracts tourists and provides employment for thousands. This is the kind of public/private partnership that is best, and I can only hope that the excessive partisanship we see today will end and cooperation and consensus can develop in the public interest. I instituted Listening Sessions in communities throughout the state and in that way uncovered ideas for community improvement. Many of these initiatives are still bearing fruit."

What did the women's movement accomplish?

"Women still do not receive equal pay, but we have women in the military (a fear often used by opponents of change during the 70s) and women climbing the ladder of large corporations. We always had the Marie Sklodowska Curies but now we have many more working in research, science, classrooms in colleges and throughout society that can only hold promise for greater accomplishments to come."

For the pharmacists' daughter, music continues to be a source of pleasure and joy. She attends opera and concerts "as often as I can," and since she now has "more time for leisure" as she approaches her 80th birthday, she decided to treat herself to a subscription to Rochester's Eastman Theatre. This lovely treasure house of beautiful music seems a fitting reward for a life well-lived. Sto lat, Mary Anne. Sto lat.[1]

1 *Sto lat* is the traditional Polish birthday greeting. Literally translated, it means "a hundred years!"

Sources:

Email correspondence with Mary Anne Krupsak.

NNDB: Tracking the Entire World, http://www.nndb.com /people/400/000206779/; University of Rochester, River Campus Libraries, http://www.lib.rochester.edu/index.cfm? page=4001.

"Carey's Legacy Fondly Remembered," *Finger Lakes Times*, August 9, 2011, p. 1A.

Linda C. Wisniewski is a native of Amsterdam. She also attended Mary Anne's elementary school, St. Stanislaus, on Cornell Street, and graduated from Amsterdam High School. She lives in Bucks County, PA where she writes for a weekly newspaper and teaches memoir workshops. Her memoir, *Off Kilter*, was published in 2008.

From Polish Immigrant to American Citizen: The Life and Letters of John C. Mazur

Daniel T. Weaver

John C. Mazur, Panama 1927.

By September 3, 1941 when John C. Mazur, age 32, received Certificate of Naturalization #5200661, he had already served in the United States Army in Panama from June 1927-June 1930 and had spent several years in the Civilian Conservation Corps. He would serve in the United States Army again during World War 2, this time as an American citizen.

Mazur was born on April 23, 1909 according to his Ellis Island Record or March 23, 1909 according to his Preliminary Form For A Declaration Of Intention. Both forms agree, however, that he was born in Harbin, Manchuria, when the Czar of Russia, for whom Mazur's father worked, ruled Manchuria.

Like many immigrants, John Casmer Mazur was not the name he was born with. Furthermore due to variant spellings, the names Mazur was known by were numerous. He was born Constantine Dembrofski or Konstantyn Dombrowski. His father was Kasimir Dombrowski and his mother was Bronslawa Zawadski. Later his last name was changed to his step-father's last name, Mazurajtis. His step-father, Peter, and his mother would later shorten their last name to Mazur. Mrs. Mazur would change her name from Bronslawa to Bernice. According to a Schenectady County Clerk's Office Census Report of June 1, 1915, however, John Mazur's name was Kostanti Mazuroite. In any event, from September 3, 1941 on, his official name was John Casmer Mazur.

Mazur's mother and step-father's last foreign address was Kovno in Lithuania. According to an 1897 Russian census, Kovno was 35% Jewish, 26% Russian, 23% Polish and only 6% Lithuanian. Along with four-year-old John, his parents emigrated to America, embarking from Rotterdam, Holland on the Holland-American Lines ship, the Ryndam.

While Mazur listed his Race as Lithuanian and his Nationality as Russian in his Declaration of Intent, it would appear that while he was born in Russian controlled territory, and his step-father was Lithuanian, both of his natural parents were Polish.

They arrived in New York City just before Christmas on December 16, 1913, headed for an uncle's house in Schenectady. The uncle, John Symonowicz, would eventually change his last name to Symon and move to RD 2 Scotia. In 1939 when Mazur was thirty-years-old and filed his intention to become a citizen, his address too was RD 2 Scotia. Eventually, his parents would move on to Rochester.

The above provides the bare bones of Mazur's life; his letters, numbering in the hundreds, and now in the possession of his daughter, Patricia Mazur Wojturski of the Town of Amsterdam, put flesh on his bones. Mazur had a gift for writing interesting letters to his parents and girlfriend, Vanda who would become his wife on Armistice day, November 11, 1939.

Mazur's letters are not those of a famous man who made world transforming decisions. His letters are those of the common man, who although born in another country, had completely embraced American values, although we must be careful to remember that most American values are not exclusively American but are universal.

The most important thing a reader comes away with after reading Mazur's letters is how much he valued family—at first his mother, step-father and sister and later on his wife and son. Related to that is his repeated references to wanting to buy a house as soon as he gets home from the war, with a nice kitchen for Vanda. And while he rarely complains in his letters, he maintains the G.I.'s right to occasionally gripe about the way the government, he is fighting to preserve, treats him.

Unfortunately, censorship had a dampening effect on Mazur's letters during World War 2. In a letter from Assam,

India dated October 27, 1944, he says, "The trouble about writing from here is that many things are censored which would make writing more interesting. So it all boils down to something like this: "Hello, I am well, hope you are the same, please write often, good by." You would be surprised to know how many letters I had returned to me for some reason or other."

In 1945, he was finally allowed to tell Vanda a little bit more about where he was and what he was doing.

"We are permitted to say that we are with the 14th Air Force and members of Randall's West China Raiders. Sounds impressive doesn't it. Well, I knew about the 14th Air Force, but for being a member of Randall's Raiders is a surprise to me as it is to you. The only raiding I've done here was to carry out an extra sandwich from the mess hall or a packet full of cookies if they didn't weigh too much."

Even with censorship in place, when he wrote about the people and places where he was stationed in China, India and Burma, his letters could be colorful.

On May 11, 1945, he wrote from China:

"Here is something you may not believe. Today we shot a stray mangy dog that was hanging around our tent. Well, it wasn't but a few minutes when a chinese woman came out of her straw shack which

John Mazur on right with friend in Asia during WW 2.

is but a stones throw away from us, to see what the shooting was about. When she saw the dead dog she made for it, and fast. She took it by the tail and dragged it away to her hut. In a few minutes the dog was skinned and quartered and what a brisk business she had selling meat. Now when she sees a dog she wants us to shoot it, including our mascot."

Mostly, however, he wrote about how much he loved and missed his wife and young son, Pete.

It is John Mazur's letters from CCC camps, when he was a younger, unmarried man, that make for the most interesting reading. Mazur was stationed at numerous camps in the west, from which he wrote home frequently.

From October 26, 1935 to September 30, 1937, Mazur was a truck driver at CCC Camp S-133 in Margaretville, NY. Mazur wrote fewer letters from Margaretville as he was close enough to home to visit.

Dana Galusha writes about the Margaretville CCC Camp in *Another Day, Another Dollar: The Civilian Conservation Corps in the Catskills* in a chapter titled, "Working Hard So Others Could Play." The title accurately describes what men like Mazur did. They built campsites and lean tos, carved ski trails and bike paths out of the woods, restored stream banks and planted hundreds of thousands of trees to restore forests that had been destroyed by the logging industry. Camp S-133 made the Catskills into a desirable place for people to get away to. Mazur arrived at the Margaretville Camp the very day it went into operation and stayed until about a year before it closed.

While the letters below, transcribed exactly as written, were not written from the Margaretville Camp, they are some of John Mazur's best letters and undoubtedly are representative of many CCCer's experiences.

Fort Lewis (?) CCC Camp July 19, 1934.

June 17 – 34

Fort Lewis.

My Dear Uncle – Auntie & Jen:

I am sorry that I did not write for so long time but I am driving an Army truck and I am traveling all the time. Just now – I drove from [illegible] to Fort Lewis 160 miles. I will stay till the 26th or 27th of this month. I quit driving the tractor. It is hard driving a little dangerous, and they won't pay more. I go to work abut 7AM and come in about 6 or 7P.M. By that time the cooks are out and have to eat cold left overs. Just like Mr. Singleton, want plenty of work done but no pay. That is the U.S. Forestry Service.

The "Westerners" take the best jobs and pay here. We are "Easterners" greenhorns out here. I saw some of the Expert Woodsman fall trees, nothing special to that. I can cut a tree down with an ax, better than some of the Westerners. I like to work for the Army. I travel all over, bring supplies to all camps, go to different cities, for food, etc. take the boys to town, in other words, driving all the time. If I drive a long ways, I can stop any place for my meals. This last trip it took me 7 hours to get over the mountains to Fort Lewis. As I am writing this letter, I see Mt. Rainier, It is beautiful, so big, and tall 12,000 ft. high. The snow on top, sparkles like diamonds. The trees here are from 100-200 ft tall, and about 5-6 ft in diameter. The air is sweet with the scent of pines, and Fir trees. The air is very thin here. All I can say is, just gorgeous. I must go to dinner now.

This is what we had. Cream of corn soup and crackers, Breaded Pork-chops, Mashed Potatoes, Cream gravey, Buttered Asparagrass, Lettice with Maynoise, Plain-cake-ice cream Bread-Butter, Fresh Milk. What do you think Just once a week though. on Sunday.

The rest of the week we have good meals. The U.S. Forestry Service don't eat like this. We have a dance every Friday nite. I get the breaks, Because my truck has a canvas top so I go to Rosyln or [illegible] to bring the girls to the camp, for the dance. But I can't dance so I go to bed or read till its time to take them back.. Have some fun though.

I haven't felt good the last couple of days. My chest bothers me. Maybe from the cold I had. Went to the hospital to be examined, but they did not say anything so I guess I'll be alright.

How is uncle getting along. Is he working the Farm? If he is what is he doing? Buy a horse? Does he feel good? How is the Rye coming? How is old Jim & Zelmo?

Well! Well! Well! And How is Dear Mom? Is she in good health? Does she still think of me? I bet she works hard. Tell her to take it easy. When she gets the money tell her to fix her teeth, buy some nice clothes. I will stay here for a long time I guess. So the money will be going home steady. Tell her and Uncle to use it, and not to save it for me. I'm young, and have plenty of time to make more. That why I'm here. To help them. I'm not as bad as I acted at home. I got a heart to. P.S. No stone either. I miss you all terribly. Especially ma good old mom! I hope she lives to be a hundred. Same of uncle and you Jen. Oh yes I didn't get my mail yet since 2 weeks. Being on the road all the times is hard to get mail. I bet I have some from home, waiting.

I am sorry that I can't buy a post-card or bottle of the xxx for Uncle's Birth-day the 24th But tell him to buy a quart of good stuff and celabrate. I must close now. I will write again on the 24th of June. Address all my mail to camp, as always.

Love to all.

John

P,S, I will write more now. I will send pictures, etc. too.

Are you working yet Jen? How is your Health?

There are to many deaths and accidents here to suit me kid, especially in Forest fires.

Date-Aug. 1, 1934
Time 7:30 P.M.
Place-Wenachi-One Hell of a Place 78 miles from state road.

Dear Folks:

Please don't expect any mail from me for some time, because I have not the time to do so. I am lucky that I can send this out. I bummed the stamps and material from our Lt. Captain. We are fighting a terrible forest fire. We are working in 2 shifts, 12 hours shifts. We have been called out 2 oclock in the morning on the 23rd of July. I drove my truck in the convoy. 78 miles of Hell, honest. The fire was on a mountain 7000 ft. above sea level. We made our own roads as we went, built small bridges, pushed burning trees and logs out of our way.

One place 2 trucks broke down, fire on all sides, smoke is terrible, noise and screams of all kinds, from animals, poor things many burned to death. A flock of sheep about 500, burned up. The boys are all tired. The fire burned up 3000 acres of woods. It is terrible to see, you just can't imagine how it looks. We had very little to eat because we can't get the supplies through fast enough. the fire is now under control. But there is a big fire in Spokane, Wash., about (300) miles from us. We will perhaps go there. They are sending men up there from all camps. We have here about 600 men. It is very fortunate no one was hurt or killed. Some had very close calls. Lightining started this fire. Oh gee, there are big fires in Idaho, California, and Oregon. The nights are cold like in Winter, we are back of the fire now. We have one blanket to 1 man. I couldn't sleep, it was too cold. We have now 6 blankets to 1 man, much better. Any way we have had very little sleep, hardly anything to eat. I will never forget this July. Big trees, 4-5 ft thick about 175 ft high burn up like a match. You know that pine tar (saps) burns like gas.

I am taking good care of my self, so don't worry. The worst thing in the world is fire, believe me. I didn't get any letters yet. No body has yet. Won't take chances on the mail being lost or burned I think. Oh hell you think. I am tired, oh yes the coffee is so strong that every time you take a drink, you move a foot. I wish I had just one of your oat-meal cookies here

now. (I got a sharp ax here)? When I ever get home tell you how we fight the fires. It takes too much space just now. My thoughts for uncle X, (Dear Mommy) X Jen X Zelmo too. Please write to main camp as always
(Casey)

P.S. How is Wanda?

I hope that you can read this alright. Tell Uncle & Ma I think of them Please buy them a radio for Xmas for me and from my (Caseys) pay. Will you? Good by & good Luck? Until you hear from me again.

(We have areo-planes drop our food orders.)

Aug 25-34
Twisp, Wash
Chilan National Forest

    I am just writing a short letter to tell you that I am at a big fire. We left on the night of Aug. 22, 3 A.M. and arrived at the scene of the fire Aug. 23, 8P.M. We have six trucks on the convoy. I was the only Army Driver from [illegible]. There are 400 men fighting fire. The men have to walk 5 miles straight up the Mt. The fire covers 3000 acres. Think that over Uncle, and its getting from under controll. The District Ranger sent in a call for 1000 men, in a hurry. We have 4 men injured, 1 badly. Camp Boulder has 9 men hurt, 1 dead. Camp Gold Creek has 1 man injured. Most injuries are caused by burns and falling rock. On the Mt. where the fire is, the rocks get so hot that they explode, and come down like bullets, some weigh 500 lbs.
    All I do is drive to this town 35 miles for food, then bring it back. We have packers take the things on horses. It is hot as hell. Don't worry I'll take care of my self. Mom knows that I am awful careful. Don't you worry ol Dear X. I took some pictures, but I don't think that they will come out. My camera got burned a little.
    Love and Kisses to all.

Casey

P.S. We are 30 miles from Canada "Border."
Wish me luck.?
            goodby-

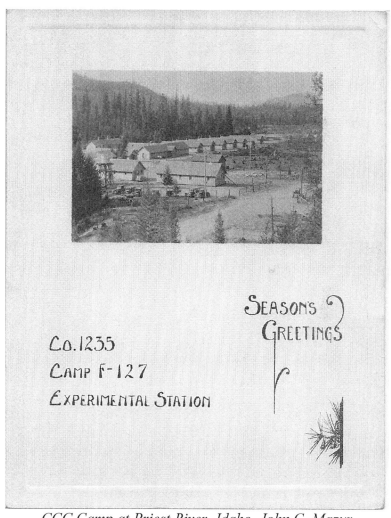

*CCC Camp at Priest River, Idaho. John C. Mazur
Collection.*

Socialist Realism, Bottom Dog Novel or Stereotypical Portrayal of Polish-Americans: Three Views of Joseph Vogel's *Man's Courage*.

Editor's Note: If we were to ask people what the best Mohawk Valley novels of all time were, surely *Drums Along the Mohawk* (1939) by Walter Edmonds, *The Damnation of Theron Ware* (1896) by Harold Frederic and *Mohawk* (1986), *The Risk Pool* (1988) and *Nobody's Fool* (1993) by Richard Russo would be among the top contenders. I would add a lesser known work, *Man's Courage* (1938), by Utica native Joseph Vogel, to the list. The following essays present three different views of *Man's Courage*. For those who haven't read it, and I recommend you do, here is a short summary from *Kirkus Reviews*.

"...this ironical, sober, simply told story of commonplace people, a Polish family, has a certain strength. Anton Wolak, simple, ignorant, inarticulate, but not without basic stamina and pride, who has always wanted to leave the city and be a farmer, but who, jobless, spends his $80.00, saved during 18 years over here, to keep going -- and then turns to relief. After weeks of useless questioning, they get relief, only to be taken off it because he gets two days of work which he neglected to report to the bureau. A worn-out wife, a child with rheumatic fever from undernourishment, the only kind of work offered him was to be a scab -- which he turns down. Finally eviction which he fights; the police are brought in and Anton is killed by a policeman shooting unnecessarily." *Kirkus Reviews*

A Man's Courage?

John Guzlowski, PhD

For a long time, I was looking forward to reading Joseph Vogel's *A Man's Courage*. From what I had heard and read about it, it was one of the only old novels that gave voice to the Polish-American experience. I could easily believe that. When I first started working in 1973 toward my PhD in American Literature, I wanted to focus on Polish-American writers. I thought that probably there were many such writers, and that this would be a rich and personally satisfying direction given my own immigrant roots, and so I asked the professors in my English Department at Purdue about Polish-American Literature.

And what did they say?

Nothing.

For all their considerable knowledge, they couldn't tell me about any books about the Polish-American experience.

And what did they do then?

They shrugged.

So I asked the other students in the program, and they had the same response. Even the ones who were five and seven years into the program couldn't tell me much. They hadn't heard about any Polish-American writers; none had been mentioned in the classes they took. Finally, when I went looking for Polish-American writing at the library, one of the preeminent American research libraries, I couldn't find anything there either.

Of course, I wasn't the only one who noticed this. In 1988, the great Polish-American scholar Stanislaus A. Blejwas wrote an impassioned essay for *Polish American Studies* called "Voiceless Immigrants" in which he deplored the absolute lack of Polish-American writers and discussed why this literature "does not exist."

Blejwas's remarks came almost 25 years ago and my own epiphany about how there was no Polish-American Lit almost forty years ago. Thankfully the situation in regards to Polish-American Literature has changed radically. A grad student at any American university can now Google Polish-

American writers and get 13,700,000 hits. (Tomorrow, there will probably be about 14,000,000 hits.) The first hit, of course, will be for the Polish-American entry at Wikipedia. There he or she will read about the considerable accomplishments of various Polish-American writers, such as the poets Phil Boiarski, Linda Nemec Foster, Hedwig Gorski, Leonard Kress, John Minczeski, Cecilia Woloch, Mark Pawlak, and yours truly, and the fiction writers Anthony Bukoski, Stuart Dybek, Leslie Pietrzyk, Thad Rutkowski and Suzanne Strempek Shea. (By the way, one of these writers, Stuart Dybek, author of a series of stories about Polish-Americans living in Chicago, recently received a MacArthur Genius Award.) Also, if you go to the online member directory for the professional organization Poets and Writers (www.pw.org) and type Polish American into the browser, you'll come up with almost a hundred members who self-identify as being, at least in part, Polish American.

But that's not all. There are plenty of writers who aren't included in the Wikipedia entry and who aren't members of Poets and Writers, who write about the Polish-American experience, and all of these writers together are writing novels, film scripts, plays, poems, and short stories about the Polish-American experience in all of its variety and complexity, its sorrows and joys, its successes and failures. In fact, I can easily tick off a list of fifty more first-rate Polish-American writers than included in the Wikipedia entry, but I won't because dozens of other Polish-American writers may wonder why I forgot to mention their names.

If Stanislaus A. Blejwas were alive today, he would probably be putting the finishing touches on an impassioned essay for *Polish American Studies* entitled "Full-Throated Immigrants."

So what does all of this have to do with Joseph Vogel and his Great Depression-era novel, *Man's Courage*? Without my knowing it back then when I was in grad school, it was one of the novels I was looking for but wasn't able to find when I started my quest for a PhD in American Literature. Of course, I didn't want those books just to help me get my PhD. I wanted to discover Vogel's novel and similar works about the Polish-American experience because they were the novels and poems and plays that I hoped would explain to me what I was as a

Polish-American immigrant and what my chances were as this kind of immigrant.

I was your archetypal immigrant. Born in a refugee camp in Germany to Polish parents, landing with them at Ellis Island in 1951, making my way westward toward Chicago with my family, angling toward some kind of success and security, I always felt estranged, isolated, alienated from the larger non-Polish culture around me. I felt odd.

I felt my language was odd, my clothes were odd, the way I did my work was odd, the way I prayed was odd. We were immigrants and DPs, Displaced Persons. And there were people who looked at us in Chicago where we finally settled like we were vermin. We got some of this surprisingly from older Polish immigrants, and we got this from some non-Poles too. I remember walking around with my father looking for rooms to rent on Milwaukee Avenue in Chicago and having people turn us away when they heard we were DPs. They told us that DP stood for Dirty Polacks and that we were drunkards, wife beaters, bar fighters, and criminals.

I'm not sure now why this was, and I wasn't sure then when I was four and five years old why it was. I would have thought that people would have been sympathetic to the recent Polish immigrants, aware of the kinds of trials and struggles they had experienced in the slave labor and concentration camps of World War II, but maybe I'm being naive. People probably just saw us as another problem, guys and gals after their jobs on the assembly lines at the Motorola and Zenith plants on the Northwest side of Chicago or down at the docks in Calumet City or Navy Pier.

I hoped that the Polish-American writers I was looking for in grad school would help me understand why we were treated this way. I hoped that a writer like Joseph Vogel in his novel *Man's Courage* would help me understand who I was and why people treated my family the way they did.

Man's Courage at first sight seemed to be just the book I needed to sort things out. Here's a brief description of the novel from the "Editor's Note":

"Set in Utica, New York (thinly disguised as 'Genesee' in Oneida County) during the Great Depression, the novels details the futile struggle of the simple Polish immigrant Adam Wolak to find what he could not have back home, a decent piece of land of his own to maintain his family. Adam's physical strength, moral soundness, and ready belief in this country's announced values are thwarted by petty bureaucrats, cheats, and ethnic ward politics. His end, which signifies the failure of his attempt to achieve personal happiness in this land of individual enterprise, leads to a rally of thousands, which signifies not only that public outrage may eventually prevail where private effort is quickly stymied but also that Adam's dream lives on. To the authorities, this man may have been a nuisance only, but to the demonstrators and the reader, he is Adam, the first human being, looking for the courage to live."

Adam is every immigrant's vision of him or herself, "the first human being." He's apparently strong, determined, morally sound, and living only for his simple, decent dream, a dream that's obstructed by political and social institutions which should know better.

With interest and growing enthusiasm, I read on past the "Editor's Note" and past Vogel's "Preface" until the first extended scene, one in which Adam Wolak visits his son's principal, Mr. Brown. He has slapped Adam's son for coming to school in ragged clothes. In the principal's office, Adam at first is "uncertain" and "angry" about what he should do, but then "his anger turns playful." He grabs Mr. Brown by his shirt, pushes him out a window, and suspends him fifty feet above the pavement.

At first, I thought that Adam's response was, to say the least, unexpected, but the way Vogel turns anger and uncertainty into playfulness suggested that Adam was something more than a very unpleasant character. He was a rounded character in the tradition of all the great characters, rife with contradictions waiting to be resolved through character development. But this momentary speculation quickly gave way to my growing sense that Adam in fact is an unpleasant character, a flat one at that.

In the next few pages, I read about Wolak's pondering that maybe the slap his son Stephen received wasn't such a bad idea. "After all," Adam reasons, "was it not time for a boy of his age to take a slap or two? No harm could come alone from that. A slap could teach one as much as books; it could teach one that there are people in superior positions who are always slapping, and people in inferior positions who are always being slapped, and among the latter only too few who return every slap with a smash." We also learn that Adam has a strained relationship with his wife and son. Adam found out about the slapping incident from a neighbor rather than from either his wife Marya or his son because he seldom talks to them. We're told that "never, never did either of them tell him of anything that happened." Finally, we learn that he will not tell his family what he did to the principal because, since they won't talk to him, he will be "ten times as stubborn" and not talk to them either.

As the novel goes on, the uncommunicative, unthinking, furious, violent side of Adam's nature is shown repeatedly, while his playfulness disappears almost immediately. Adam is continuously depicted as taciturn, angry, violent, sexually attracted to his landlord's young daughter, unthinking, almost illiterate, unable to speak to others, isolated from his wife and son. When he gets frustrated while trying to apply for relief, he rushes forward and grabs a clerk. A security guard and three policemen escort Adam from the relief agency. Later, while drinking he gets into a fight with two guys who might be trying to enlist his help in a burglary. As one of the guys smashes his fist into Adam's face, Adam comes alive: "From Adam's chest burst a roar. The fists beating into his face felt good: ah, they felt good! He grasped the young man's neck, pushed him backward, forced him up against the partition, and banged his head against the wood – banged it and banged it, and from his chest came out a roar of fury and joy." When his son gets terribly sick and Adam's wife Marya tries to leave the house to get help, Adam locks her in her room. When Marya pleads for him to let her go, Adam says, "Go to hell, that's where I'll let you go."   Describing this impasse with his wife to a casual acquaintance in a bar over a few drinks, Adam shouts, "She no goddam good! By Jesus, I smash her to pieces."

As the novel progresses and Adam's financial situation worsens, he moves increasingly toward anger and violence. All of this culminates of course, in the scene where the marshal comes to evict Adam's family from the house they are renting at that point. With Marya screaming, Adam breaks a chair over the marshal and then grabs an unloaded rifle. Soon the police arrive, and Adam dies when he's shot by a police officer for refusing to put down his rifle.

I read this and wonder what am I supposed to think. I sought out this book to find out who as an immigrant I am and why I was treated the way I was, and what I discover is a character, Adam Wolak, who appears to be the sort of fellow people thought my father and me and all the other Displaced Persons, all the other Polish immigrants were: a brutal, unthinking, violent animal. The people who refused to rent us even a single room along Milwaukee Avenue when we first came to America as DPs were apparently doing the right thing. If they had rented us an apartment, there would have been the devil to pay and the police to call.

What's going on?

What's going on is that Vogel is writing not about Polish Americans but rather about a stereotype, the brute figure so often seen in the Naturalistic writing of the late 19th century and early 20th century. He's the kind of character you encounter in Frank Norris's *Vandover and the Brute* and *McTeague*, in Stephen Crane's *Maggie: A Girl of the Streets* and "The Blue Hotel," in Eugene O'Neill's *Hairy Ape* and *The Emperor Jones*. The brute heroes and heroines in these works live short, violent lives that often end in predictably brutal deaths. These characters were used to some extent to support the validity of a Naturalistic view of life as being, according to the famous formulation of literary historian Donald Pizer, pessimistic, materialistic, and deterministic. What Vogel is offering is a type rather than a person, and as a type Adam Wolak finally isn't very engaging, and he doesn't answer the types of questions about the Polish-American immigrant's life that I'm hoping to find in the pages of Vogel's *Man's Courage*.

In fact, Vogel's work with its adherence to Naturalism plays into a lot of the anti-Polish stereotypes that we see in Polish jokes and anti-Polish attitudes. Adam Wolak is the Pole who can't unscrew the light bulb, can't figure out the relief system, can't talk to his wife, can't figure out how to talk to a police man or a priest, can't get along with his best friend, can't get the available free medical care for his son who has pneumonia, can't get a job shoveling snow because he threw away his shovel.

I'm not saying that there were no Polish Americans like the ones Vogel writes about in *Man's Courage*. There were. I grew up in an immigrant neighborhood in Chicago, and I still shake my head over some of the craziness and brutality I witnessed. But the drunk neighbor beating his son with a belt and then stripping off his clothes and running through the streets was the exception not the norm. Vogel focuses on this kind of sensationalism to get his point across, but that point seems flat and predictable in the context of contemporary Polish-American writers. To see some real Poles, round characters who are psychologically motivated and capable of thinking their way through their motivation, I'd need to read works by actual Polish-Americans not in the thrall of Naturalism. I'd have to read writers like Phil Boiarski, Anthony Bukoski, Stuart Dybek, Linda Nemec Foster, John Minczeski, Christina Pacosz, Mark Pawlak, Leslie Pietrzyk, Susan Strempke Shea, John Surowiecki, Thad Rutkowski, and Cecilia Woloch.

John Guzlowski was born the son of parents who met in a slave labor camp in Nazi Germany. He grew up in Chicago's immigrant and DP neighborhoods. Guzlowski earned his PhD in English at Purdue University in 1980, and is now retired from Eastern Illinois University, where he taught contemporary American literature and poetry writing. His poems deal with his parents' experiences as slave laborers in Nazi Germany. He has authored two books: *Lightning and Ashes* and *Third Winter of War: Buchenwald* (Finishing Line Press). He blogs about the Polish Diaspora at http://writingpolishdiaspora.blogspot.com/

Epitaph on a Literary Genre: Socialist Realism and Joseph Vogel's *Man's Courage*

L. D. Davidson

It was good times. It was bad times. Well, it was more bad than good. It was the 1930's, the time of the Great Depression. Whether one was a working class person in upstate New York, in the Soviet Union of Stalin, or in Germany when Hitler was consolidating power, it was hard times. It was hard times nearly everywhere.

It was also a decade of illusions. On the spectrum of public illusion, perhaps no greater illusion infected otherwise enlightened people than the illusion that the Soviet Union under Joseph Stalin represented the best opportunity for a just world. Not many individuals were as perceptive as George Orwell who had recognized as early as the mid 1930's that Stalinism AND Fascism, BOTH represented grave menaces. Among the American sympathizers of Stalinist style Communism, many individuals would later come to repent their earlier naivety.

Joseph Vogel was another of the many early admirers of working class socialism. His 1939 novel *Man's Courage* set in Utica remains a curious period piece of American political literature written on the backside of his enthusiasm for Socialism. Vogel's novel does indeed possess some historical relevancy today because it is emblematic of the viewpoint of so many 1930's U.S. radicals.

In order to understand Vogel's novel, it is important to place the novel within its specific historical context. The assassination of Kirov in 1934 marks the beginning of the great Soviet purges. Trotsky was by then living in exile. Other former colleagues of Stalin in the Soviet leadership had been discredited and executed. The gulag system had begun swallowing Soviet humanity, having claimed by 1939, among many other victims, prominent literary men like Osip Mandelstam and Maxim Gorky. In the midst of this Stalinist purge, two other developments disillusioned the American adherents of Stalinist Socialism. First, some of the leftist veterans of the Spanish Civil War, among them Dos Passos, George Orwell and Arthur Koestler, began publicizing the duplicitous actions of the Communists in Spain. Betrayals, assassinations and infighting among the supporters of the Republican government in Spain led to the victory of Franco. Many other Anglo-American leftists had begun bitterly complaining about the lack of support they had received in Spain from their Communist allies. The second event, a huge psychological blow to American leftists, occurred on August 21, 1939 when the Soviet Union signed a non-aggression pact with Nazi Germany. This Molotov-Ribbentrop Pact, which was the prelude to the invasion of Poland by Nazi Germany, further embittered many Communist sympathizers.

In the immediate wake of these events, Vogel's novel was published by Knopf. Most of the novel had been written before Vogel had become aware of the facts about Stalinist reality. In many ways this novel is a last hurrah, not only for Vogel's promising literary career, but also for the genre of social realist literature in the United States. Soon after its publication, the necessity of opposing Nazi Germany, and then, after the war, the developing Cold War tensions forced U.S. leftists far to the periphery of U.S. culture. Many U.S. leftists were demoralized, and the evidence indicates that Joseph Vogel, at least as a literary writer, was disillusioned enough that he worked only half-heartedly on a further novel before abandoning creative literature for social work. Then, the publication in 1940 of Koestler's *Darkness At Noon* made Vogel's novel of 1939 seem politically naïve.

This is now a very misunderstood novel. It is decidedly not a regional novel of ethnic immigrant experience. Adam Wolak, the main character, may be a Polish immigrant, but he is far more true to typical socialist stereotypes. It is probably true that the advocates for this novel must try to position it as a regional novel of regional ethnic experience, if it is going to become more than a minor footnote in 20th American literature. Nevertheless, such a misrepresentation distorts the novel's raison d'etre.

Adam Wolak is a fictional creative stereotype of the socialist worker. He epitomizes a kind of suppressed vitality. He is a man with a poor education, a worker possessing virile strength, who has been victimized by the impersonal forces of capitalism. Eastern European towns and museums were filled with idealized statues of Adam Wolak-like figures—Wolak as WWII hero, Wolak, the loyal factory worker, Wolak celebrating with his family the electrification of a village. And isn't that basically Adam Wolak in Bela Uitz' Communist Party placards? In numerous versions of those street placards Wolak, the apotheosis of the idealized working man, proudly carries the red flag at the head of a surging mob of triumphant workers. As a creative artist, though, it is the Hungarian artist Gyula Derkovits who did more textured representations of exploited workers in his paintings from the 1930's. As it is, Adam Wolak cannot possibly be mistaken for anything other than a clichéd figure—an ideological type, unmistakable whether he is portrayed in Budapest, St Peterburg, Warsaw or Utica. Wolak is not just a Polish immigrant in Utica in the 1930's. That is just a convenient setting drawn from Vogel's personal experience. For all Vogel cares, Wolak could be Italian or Irish or Yahooian. The point is what Wolak represents from the perspective of the international Socialist movement. He is a character who is trans-ethnic and trans-regional.

But to recognize that Vogel is writing within the clichés of social realism—and the examples in this novel are numerous, from the scene of the public reading of the letter about the death of Wolak's brother in the Austrian Civil War to the characterization of Wolak's wife and sick son—is not to say that Wolak is a forgettable character in the evolution of the American novel. It is certainly true that George Buchner had created the prototype for Adam Wolak in his play *Woyzeck*. Buchner was writing more than one hundred years before Vogel created his Wolak. Buchner created Woyzeck with more depth, as a character whose despair is fuelled by a passion for a woman much more vivid than the one-dimensional Marya is.

Vogel's Wolak is a character completely at the mercy of economic forces he cannot control. The impersonal forces arrayed against him are one-dimensional abstractions. Miss Lyons, the relief agency worker, and Mrs. Janis, the citizenship teacher, and D'Amico, the ward politician, are likewise one-dimensional characters without any hint of a layered inner life. Moreover, the relationship between Rose and Adam is an attraction without a clear romantic logic. Rose herself is another one-dimensional character and her interest in Adam has a

Gerichtsbescheid (Court Order). Gyula Derkovitz.

cartoonlike quality. The larger point is that Vogel's characters are—to a great extent—just caricatures. They are flat, one-dimensional figures on the socio-economic landscape of the Great Depression.

Even taking into account this novel's limitations, it is also fair to note how remarkably "un-regional" it is in its perspective. Vogel is surprisingly well-informed about the Austrian Civil War of the 1930's. If he were searching in the 1938-1939 period—as he must have been—for a credible Socialist alternative to Stalinist Communism, then Austro-Marxism did indeed offer a promising alternative. How did a Utica-born, locally educated person know so much about the 1934 Austrian Civil War?

Bottom Section of Menschheit (Humanity), 1920. Bela Uitz.

Vogel was indeed astonishing well informed about details such as the Austrian Schutzbund and the betrayal of Otto Bauer and some other Austrian Socialist leaders. In fact, at times, Adam Wolak resembles a 1930's character right out of an evening Volkshochschule class in Vienna's Meidling district. The depth of understanding in the letter announcing the death of Adam's brother is rich in detail and accurate in its interpretation of the situation in Austria in 1934. Such details provide historical context of high quality and they lend this novel an unusual depth .

Very few novels of this variety exist on the surface of American literature. But it is by no means surprising at all that Joseph Vogel was eclipsed in the big American backlash against socialist culture in the late 1940's and 1950's. Even so, *Man's Courage* remains an interesting period novel. But is Vogel anything like an American Zola? Hardly. Is he as original as Buchner? Not even close. Is he a regional U.S. writer? No way. Is he a worthy footnote in 20th century American literature? Certainly. Dos Passos ran out of creative juice and turned to the right after the truth about Stalinism tapped his political indignation. And Vogel? He faded into obscurity only to resurface in Ohio as an adjunct English professor in the 1960's. He died fifty-four years after he gave up fiction in the wake of his third novel.

By 1940 the truth about Stalinist reality was choking the vital force out of the American Left. It is no big riddle why *Man's Courage* must be deceptively positioned now as a novel of immigrant ethnic experience. Read it today and mourn—if you like—for the time when the possibility of working class culture could excite the imaginations of idealists--- before the old U.S. working class got just enough disposable income to move onto the living room sofa to become a passive consumer of sports entertainments. Or perhaps read it as a kind of epitaph on the death of a 20th century American literary genre. Truly, though, by the 1990's Joseph Vogel must have been a very disillusioned man.

L. D. Davidson is a Latin teacher and editor of *Antium*, a journal "rooted in reason and representing a vision of creative and intellectual substance amid the incoherence of the Present." He is also a regular contributor to the Op-Ed page of *The Sunday Gazette* and to the *Mohawk Valley Independent*. If you are interested in *Antium*, you can contact Davidson through *Upstream*.

An Excerpt from "Literary Visions of Ethnic History from Upstate New York" by John M. Reilly, PhD, published in *Upstate Literature Essays in Memory of Thomas F. O'Donnell*, Edited by Frank Bergmann (Syracuse: Syracuse University Press, 1985). Reprinted with the permission of Syracuse University Press.

Joseph Vogel began publishing short fiction in 1926, the year he graduated from Hamilton College. Working as a reporter on a trade paper and later as an editor of a business magazine, he made time after hours to write stories, several of which appeared in the famous American Caravan Anthologies. Like most prose writers, however, Vogel's chosen form was the novel. He reports writing and discarding four attempts at long fiction before 1935 when Alfred A. Knopf published *At Madame Bonnard's*. The reviews were everything a young writer might wish, and together with other successes showed the possibility of Vogel being very much part of the the contemporary literary scene in New York. Besides regular publication in the influential little magazines, he also secured fellowships at Yaddo in 1932 and one from the Munson-Williams-Proctor Institute in his hometown of Utica. These awards enabled him to complete his second novel, *Man's Courage*, which appeared in 1938, again as a publication by the prestigious firm of Alfred A. Knopf. There was a third novel, too, *The Straw Hat,* but by the time he completed it, Vogel had found it impossible to maintain his family any longer without full-time employment and therefore entered federal service as an employee of the Bureau of Prisons. The job was so demanding that it effectively ended his writing career until many years later, when he became a writing instructor at Ohio State University (MacDonald).

The outline of Vogel's career shows him in the familiar environment of the writer of the 1930s serving an apprenticeship among his peers, seeking with them the outlets for his creative work that are necessary to become a functioning writer if not an established one. He found sufficient success to certify his talent as genuine, but not the luck, support, or sales to enable him to survive in the mainstream of American writing, and it is important to note that his writing career does show him to be part of that mainstream.

At Madame Bonnard's, his first novel, is constructed on the pattern of the venerable group tale, recounting experiences of lodgers in a New York City rooming house. The structure is an excellent means of opening up the novel to allow rendition of a cast of particularized characters while suggesting a commonality of experience that offers suggestions of a collective identity. At one and the same time such a construction embodies the supposition of literary realism that

Genesee & Bleecker Streets. Utica. Circa 1910. Library of Congress.

character is both individual and representative and also provides the new writer readily managed access to a traditional way of telling a tale. The characters and experience could very well be ethnic, but, as the use of the group tale in war stories or disaster tales indicates, the significance of the form does not demand any commonality beyond proximity. It would require the application of a writer's specialized purpose to convert the form into support of an ethnic theme.

That specialized purpose appears in Vogel's second novel, *Man's Courage*, which displays Polish-American ethnicity in the development of the character of the protagonist Adam

Wolak, a massive man whose dependence on physical strength and elemental love of nature links him to the peasantry. Resident for eighteen years in Genesee—that is, Utica—Adam is presented with the opportunity to become a citizen of the United States by Mrs. Janis, a political appointee of Alderman D'Amico, whose interest in helping immigrants rests on the addition they can make to the numbers of voters indebted to him. The lessons Mrs. Janis gives Adam are patronizingly simplistic. She explains, for example, that America is not a democracy but a republic: "A Democracy is direct rule by the masses, and when you have such a government you can be sure you have no respect for life and property, what you have is mobocracy. A Republic, on the other hand, is a representative form of government, where representatives are duly elected for their capability, and when you have that, as opposed to government by the masses, then you have respect for law, justice, and progress" (65). The reason for making the point about a republic, Mrs. Janis assures Adam, is to show him how fortunate he is. Unlike a native-born American, he does not have to live twenty-one years under the government before he can vote. "Just think, an uneducated immigrant comes here from the old country, where all he knew was poverty and misery, and after only five years he can enjoy the full privileges of citizenship" (65-66). And, in the example of Genesee, the first ward of which is represented by Joseph D'Amico. "He's a wonderful man! He has accomplished marvels for the first ward!" (66)

The parody of American civics lessons is matched by the satiric representation of Adam's experiences in the relief station where, since he is unemployed, he must endure the delays and misunderstandings of a bureaucracy contemptuous of those who seem unable to help themselves. Functioning to degrade and suppress people like Adam, the system is his nemesis. At each point of turn in the plot the system demeans Adam, until the legalistic demand for the eviction of his family from a low rent house results in his being shot dead by uniformed marshalls. Actually, there has been a legal error. Families with a sick child cannot be evicted, but correction of the ironic error, even if accomplished before Adam's death, would hardly soften the point that the organized agencies of society, including the church, are the foes of the ethnic hero. They have no intention of permitting him entry into complete citizenship and use their ethical and political teachings as a means of controlling the perceived threat of the people presumed to be unassimilable. On the level of plot, then, *Man's Courage* works to portray an irresolvable conflict arising from ethnic difference, a conflict that eventuates in victimization; yet for several reasons it would be inappropriate to describe Vogel's narrative as exclusively a tale of the victim.

Though he perishes in conflict, the protagonist lives a life enriched by contact with other immigrants and nurtured by his family. He is no mere brute, as those who mean to control him assume; nor is he powerless, as his fate suggests. Adam Wolk rages justifiably, sustains an ethical outlook on life that keeps him from temptation, and demonstrates a capacity for commitment to his fellows; thus he is a humanized character directed by values and feelings that give his fated end a quality of tragedy. Moreover, the narrative voice—a traditional third person—identifies with Adam's perspective so that the powerful presentation of the crushing system of organized welfare and politics is associated with the evaluation made by Adam himself. The evident parody of the citizenship lessons and the actions of the directors of relief programs, recounted with such extremity that they become satiric, appear infuriatingly ridiculous because the novel has established Adam as a dignified, worthy man. Adam may be marginal to the agencies of society, but he is the ethical norm providing the measures of conduct properly attributed to a hero.

Observation that the novel places an immigrant peasant in the role of a tragic hero within a plot of victimization does not exhaust the ethnic significance of the narrative, for *Man's Courage* works also as social criticism and, beyond that, as an exploration of the historical experience of ethnicity. The conflict between Adam and the destructive system constitutes a struggle between visions of life. The vision contained in the simplistic behavior of Mrs. Janis and the relief workers amounts to a bare ideological treatment of people. It is driven by fear of the immigrant working class to distort American political philosophy in order to justify denial of sympathy and humane treatment. It asserts the accepted notion that one's initiative can overcome adversity in order to universalize exploitations. In that respect the values of a majority society are abstracted for use as means of forestalling acceptance of the minority. In his opposing view, Adam values a fuller way of life, an ideology that has place in it for all.

Polish Strikers in Utica circa 1915.
Source Library of Congress.

The conflict between a reductionist ideology and a full way of life finds its fullest play through the provision of a special historical context for the events of Adam Wolak's life. As the novel opens, Adam has received a letter written in German and dispatched from Czechoslovakia that contains news of his brother's role in the revolt of Viennese workers against the Dollfuss government in 1934. As the letter relates events, it becomes clear that Andrew Wolak had died in a struggle betrayed by reformism. The workers' unity and heroism would have prevailed had not the leadership compromised the socialist values that instigated revolt. Since Adam does not read German he must have someone else read the letter, and, when he does, news of the glorious battle of a workers' army inspires the immigrant neighborhood and wins for Adam fame as the brother of a workers' hero. It is against the background of these events that the plot of *Man's Courage* evolves, making it clear that Adam's resistance and rage against the dehumanizing system in Genesee is an equivalent to Viennese revolt. The radical orientation provided by the letter gains reinforcement in the narrative from explanatory statements such as one on solidarity of workers presented by an organizer for unemployment councils (227-28) and from principled action such as Adam's refusal to take a job at Alderman D'Amico's business when he discovers that the unionized workers are on strike.

The effect of providing a historical context of workers' struggle is to establish the troubles faced by Adam Wolak in Genesee as part of a pattern of broader social issues: his individual experiences are cast always in collective terms. What happened to Adam is everyone's fate. Appropriately, then, after Adam's death the novel moves to its close with scenes showing how his funeral generates a collective wrath, producing in his victimization a spirit to achieve a genuinely democratic society.

John M. Reilly, PhD is a former professor of English at the University of Albany and President of United University Professions from 1987-1983 and the author of numerous articles.

My Vow: I Will Never Be an Immigrant

Danusha Goska, PhD

My final three days in Poland a movie scene kept replaying itself on the screen suspended in my mind. Especially persistent was the soundtrack of this scene, a street accordion rendition of the surpassingly wistful Piaf ballad, "La Vie en Rose." The scene is from Billy Wilder's 1954 film, S*abrina*.

Audrey Hepburn is Sabrina, beautiful, naïve, the daughter of a chauffeur, in love with a rich boy. Her father has sent her to France to learn to be a cook. It's a Golden Age film, shot in a Hollywood studio; no one in the cast got anywhere near Paris. And yet, as classic films could do, *Sabrina* evokes Paris, makes you feel Paris, more intimately and thoroughly than many a modern film shot on location.

Sabrina conjures Paris with a few, low-budget waves of a black-and-white magic wand. You see the Eiffel Tower outside the cooking school's artistically rounded, antique window. Probably no real cooking school has so crystalline and unimpeded view of the Eiffel Tower. You hear a French accent from a chef in a tall hat who sadistically ridicules failed soufflés but worships well-made ones.

I don't know if, my last few days in Poland, I was remembering the scene accurately, but this is how it kept replaying inside my head: Sabrina is seated at a desk at night. Outside her window glows the ghostly, bulbous Basilica of Sacre-Coeur, a Montmarte landmark. On the street below her window, a busker is cranking out "La Vie en Rose" from an accordion.

Sabrina sits in the spherical halo of a desk lamp. Even though this is a black-and-white film, you know the lamplight is golden. You can tell from her erect and yet comfortable posture how serene Sabrina is, and you can tell that Paris has created this inner contentment. In a voiceover, Sabrina speaks the letter she is composing to her father, the chauffeur. She has completed her schooling, and is about to return to America. She plainly is in love with Paris. She can handle leaving, though, because Paris has graced her, and she will carry that special Parisian grace within her for the rest of her life.

There are no action, no innovative camera angles, in this scene. It consists of just a few brief images, a few spare lines of script. But Wilder, Hepburn, and that damn accordion player convey so very much. Maybe it's the lyrics, or, better, the tune of "La Vie en Rose," a song that expresses bittersweet longing so very well.

How did they lure my mother onto the flowered ox cart? A necklace of flowers around the ox – just like in a pagan child sacrifice. Did they admit to her then and there that she'd never again see her beloved grandmothers, the women who showed her love, love that, by all accounts, her own mother stinted? That, like millions of other peasants, from up and down Eastern Europe, the Mediterranean, China, Japan, she was leaving the green and earth of home for America's soot and smoke? Or did they lie, as adults and life so often lie to children, and claim that it would just be a short ride, a short ride little one, you'll be back in your own bed by nightfall?

One must not romanticize the village, and peasant life, but the village my mother – that little girl – left to come to American exploitation and coal really was paradise. She had not yet put in an eighteen-hour day in the fields. She had not yet been put in her place by the powers that be, either Hungarians or aristocrats or Nazis or Soviets. Her village was blue sky, a clean river where children swam, and flowers, the cuckoo's call through dense woods, the castle, her grandfather's beehives, her father's sheep, the folksongs and the legends and the Hasterman who haunted bodies of water at night, the self-sufficiency of adults who could accomplish anything with their own bare hands, from treating tumors with garden herbs to building a house, and a love that enfolded her. She got to go to school in the village, and she scored the highest grades. She had a mind, and would accomplish impressive intellectual feats someday. She marched in pilgrimages and she was "the prettiest girl in the village."

Then the ox cart. The train station. The boat, the nauseating voyage, celery soup, soot, coal, no more school, cleaning rich people's houses. The death of dreams.

There was no return in those days, short of actual return. Phone calls were impossibly expensive. When we finally visited, I don't remember any of my relatives actually owning a phone. Phone calls were monitored by authorities on both sides of the Atlantic. There was no internet, no skype. I remember receiving censored letters. I remember receiving letters that intimated what could be said, and what could not be said.

All those memories. All that love. All that longing. All those immigrants and all those that loved them. Bottled up. Forced down. Choked back. Denied. Buried. All that energy never expressed. No wires to transmit it. Where did that energy go? Unwept tears. What dam could hold them back? My mother dreamed of walking home with her brother across the Atlantic Ocean.

My mother buried two sons who died in the prime of life, and I don't remember her crying at funerals. I remember her cleaning house in summer, 1968. I remember her suddenly stopping her work and sitting in front of the TV screen. To see my mother suddenly stopping her work? Impossible. Even more impossible was this: tears on my mother's face. On the TV screen: tanks rolling into Prague. I stood still, and looked at my mother, and felt awe. The image impressed itself into my brain, and I've never forgotten it. I learned a big lesson that day, and I can't put it into words, except these words: my mother, crying, as she watched Soviet tanks rolling into Prague.

As it happens, I was alone with her when she died. Given what was happening, given our history, there are any number of portentous items on our agenda, any number of themes my mother and I could have addressed as she exited this life. What did I do, what did I say? I swept the other themes aside. I spoke to her in Slovak. I played a cassette of Slovak folk music. I reassured her that she would soon reunite with people – grandmothers in black babushkas, chicken-thief uncles, the Jewish boy next door who saved her life when she was drowning in the river Nitra, that boy the Germans took away, her aunt who beat collaborators with her broom – I told her that she would soon reunite with these she never stopped loving and had left irrevocably, forever, decades ago.

I was stunned by how much Polish I remembered. I was stunned when people said a sentence to me, and I understood it, and then another sentence, and I understood that, as well, and then a third. I wondered if this was a trick my mind was playing on me. Before I left for Poland this summer, I considered purchasing a phrase book so that I would be able to navigate train ticket kiosks and souvenir shopping. I was stunned when I could summon not just the words and even the grammar for "My name is," "how are you," "how much does that cost" and "where is the toilet," but also for "Make yourself comfortable" and "It would be better if you could take advantage of this" and "You can order my book from Amazon." I was stunned when Poles said, "How did you know that particular, difficult grammar structure?" And I looked back and said, "No, I don't know it. I don't speak Polish at all."

Remembering Polish meant remembering my life. Remembering my life before graduate school, its horrors, the attack by the crazy professor, getting sick, being sick for years, losing my life savings, all of that evil that knocked my life completely off course. That was the last thing I did before graduate school, before doom – I went to Poland, and I studied Polish, and I decided to make some contribution to scholarship about Poles and Poland. Funny how suddenly acknowledging that you know an obscure vocabulary word, or grammatical structure, can force you into a confrontation with memories you survive by forgetting.

What would I remember if I suddenly began speaking French every day, the language I spoke in Africa? Or Nepali? I'm so intimidated by this question, I'm not even going to try.

I felt so at home in Poland. It was overwhelming. I kept waiting for the feeling to fade but it never did. I felt an at-homeness that eludes me in America. That doesn't mean I don't feel at home in America; I do. It's just a different room of home. Poland is another room. A warm, and cozy, and imperfect room. The heat is too high. I try to open the window to let some fresh air in, and the woman with the child in her lap complains. The air becomes a bit stifling. But I am familiar with, at home with, that kind of air. I remember it from childhood, from my Aunt Tetka's house: too much antique furniture, rugs, knick-knacks, curtains, yet more curtains, too many meals, too little fresh air. But very good pastry. And if you can get them to sing, and the slivovice always gets them to sing, they know all one hundred verses of the folksong.

Does the internet and the rapid electronic connection it provides make things easier? Or does it lure us onto new ox carts, into crying new tears? During this visit to Poland I met two people, Krystyna, and Malgorzata, whom, previously, I had known only from the internet, and two others whom I had known in Poland decades ago and not seen since.

One afternoon, I received, too late, a note inviting me to meet Krystyna and her daughter Nikki for dinner. I rushed to the old town, knowing I'd arrive an hour after the time she'd suggested we meet. I had little idea what she looked like, and no idea what her daughter looked like. Krakow's Rynek Glowny, main square, was thronging with tourists. I passed within four feet of two women. I stared at them. The little voice said to me, "That is Krystyna and Nikki. Greet them." I hesitated, suddenly struck dumb. I thought, that would be too weird. Approaching two strange women in this crowded square and saying – what? In what language? That my little voice told me that these were the women I was rushing to meet? The two women passed. When Krysytna, Nikki and I finally connected I realized that that indeed had been they. Whatever had transpired between Krystyna and me via the internet had created a connection strong enough that in a crowd of hundreds my path would skin hers and I would recognize her on sight.

Krystyna, Nikki and I spent pleasant time together. And then it was time for them to get their plane. I didn't want that moment to arrive. I felt so at home with both of them, these women I'd just met. I wanted them as next-door-neighbors. Given how far apart we live, I realized we might never again share a casual talk over pizza. Suddenly the reality of that separation seemed impossibly wrong. Greed: I did not want to return to just internet. I demanded in-the-flesh. As we said goodbye on Ulica Florianska, I surprised myself by crying, and by actually wanting to hug. I'm one of those non-huggers; I usually just hug out of politeness. But I wanted to hold on to Krystyna, to keep her by my side, not to let distance have her. But I had to surrender.

And, Malgorzata. We said our goodbyes Sunday night. "This is not a very sentimental goodbye," I observed. "I am not a sentimental person," Malgorzata countered. We were under Kosciol Mariacki, a medieval church. Night was falling on Europe's largest medieval square; mist was rising from the cobblestones into the stoplight-haloed air. Malgorzata, unsentimental, suddenly adjured me, "I love my country when you write about it." She turned to go. St. Mary's church bell struck the hour, and, as Malgorzata's footsteps died away down a misted Ulica Florianska, the trumpeter began the hejnal. This was Poland, and the country would insist on providing the atmosphere.

And, in Poland, I reconnected with two people I had known when I lived there during 1988-89, one a man, one a woman; two people I had not seen in two decades. The man and I had not had any contact of any kind in twenty-two years. And here we were, seated at a sidewalk café on Ulica Juliusza Lea, blueberry pastry in front of us, dry lightning parting the July sky hanging over the fruit and vegetable stalls across from us, having the same argument we had back in 1989, but using different words. I thought of a poem I had written to him that has remained ensconced in the cover of my diary; would I have the courage to speak that poem's exhortations now? No. The moment never really arrived for those words in 1989, and it would not come this afternoon. I wondered, did he realize that there was dry lightning that night 22 years ago? I did.

The hammer of my own heart and the whispered cautions of my own head were both too loud for me to register this renewed contact. He said we should meet again. I agreed. At least I would be present enough to register another encounter. But time and distance swallowed him up. We never met again. I remain in that place where the wave has taken you, and your head is over your heels, and you are waiting for the wave to pass, so your soles can nestle on ground, again. When I am once again perpendicular to earth, I will have to ask, Did we really even meet? What did we say? Was it good? Was anything resolved?

Later, I was seated on a bench outside Dom Studencki Piast, chatting with Stephanie, a gorgeous and talented writer, a young Polish-Greek American from New Jersey. "You're Polish and Greek?" I said. "You should open a diner. The Germans would invade." And suddenly there, in front of Dom Studencki Piast, was Tenia, whom I met in that very structure twenty-two years ago. Tenia was with her three children. I met their father in Dom Studencki Piast, as well. I remember his courting Tenia; I remember Beatrice Ekwa-Okoko, half

Cameroonian, half-Polish, and I vetting this man as a potential husband for Tenia, right here in Dom Studencki Piast.

Now, twenty-two years later, I jumped off the bench and embraced Tenia. We hugged. And hugged. I could hear Stephanie commenting, "That is a very long hug." The world slipped away and it was just me and Tenia. You're only supposed to say that about romantic relationships.

Tenia and I chatted. We strolled Krakow. We sought makowiec, my favorite Eastern European delicacy, pastry made of ground poppy seeds spiraled between layers of a rich dough. My mother used to instruct me in baking it, back when poppy seed was affordable and we owned a cast aluminum grinder for the seeds. Tenia ran into two friends, and they joined our strolling salon. Tenia's attention was divided. I realized that Tenia would have to cut her visit with me short, soon.

Aware of that goodbye on the horizon, I tried to cauterize the pain. I stood up. "I have to go." I thought I'd escape the bakery quickly and cleanly. Tenia followed me out onto the street. Her large eyes were red and wet. She hugged me once, two times, three – it almost became a comedy. Almost.

I returned to my dorm room and felt I'd been hit by a car. The pain didn't have any words attached. It was not, "I will miss her so much." It was not, "Remember that fight we had on that train trip to Bialystok when we ended up in Lodz."

Two of the toughest goodbyes in my life: the death of my brother Phil, and the death of my Uncle John. I sat and thought. What if I received a note, right now, stating that it had all been a mistake, that Phil or Uncle John had not really died, but had been alive this entire time, just completely inaccessible to me? And that one or the other was about to walk into the room and we were to reunite?

On the surface, one might think that such a note would bring celebratory joy. The return of something very valued, but lost. Instead, I felt a sense of utter horror. Losing both of them had been so hard. Reuniting with them would torment me. Why did we lose all those years, all those years when we could have been together? Sealing over the wound with an insensible scar was too much work. That scar is my investment, and I will remain more loyal to it than to the promise of contact that might quiver with pain.

One of my best moments during this trip to Poland. I was rushing down Ulica Karmeliczka in the early morning hours. There were not too many people on the street. A middle-aged woman, short, with short, dyed black hair, was walking toward me. She was shuffling items from her wallet. She dropped something, and moved on. Was she dropping litter? That didn't seem like a particularly Polish thing to do.

I was rushing and not focused, but I felt I had to pick up the item the woman had dropped. I glanced at it. It was the size of a credit card, and it looked official. "Prosze," I mumbled, halfheartedly. The woman kept moving away from me. "Prosze pani," I announced, more forcefully. The woman turned around. I did not move toward her; I held out the item in my hand. She walked back a few steps, focusing on my hand. Suddenly she sprang to life. "Oh!" she exclaimed. "How could I have...???" She took the item from my hand, and, never looking at me, just kept saying, "How could I have lost this?" and "Oh!"

I don't think she ever looked at me, ever realized that I was just a tourist. She had dropped something evidently important, and on the almost empty sidewalk I happened to pick it up and return it to her, in response to an inner prodding. I kept walking my way, she, hers. If I had not traveled thousands of miles to that anonymous encounter, she might have lost that important item. I don't know.

When I was a kid, witness to my mother's pain, I vowed: I will never be an immigrant. I don't drink coffee or tea. People think it's weird. They ask me why. I never tell them. Here's why: I grew up in a town full of immigrant laborers. My mother's friends would come to the house, sit around the table, drink coffee or tea, and the lament would begin. Nothing was good. All the news was bad. I remember isolated words: husbands, fathers, children, ingrates, cancer, priests, bosses, lousy, what are you going to do? There were no solutions. I swore: I'll never be an immigrant, and I'll never drink coffee or tea, because I don't want this pain.

So, I was never an immigrant. I never rode the one-way ox cart; I always purchased a round-trip ticket. But I always knew it would be my destiny to be a traveler. And that pain finds you no matter how rapidly or glamorously you move.

TO THE SEVENTH GENERATION

Stephen Lewandowski

The traditional Algonquin prescription that has also been ascribed to the Iroquois, to "consider the impact of tribal decisions to the seventh generation," threatens to become just another cliché. A company distributing "earth-friendly" products through catalogue sales has "borrowed" the name. The concept itself has been advanced in all sorts of forums, and its goal of promoting careful consideration of the full and long-term consequences of actions is worthy. It works well with consensus decision-making but not as well with win-lose majority rule, which continues to be the most common political mode in the United States.

That said, what is the length of time implied in the original formula? How long is "to the seventh generation?" Like many concepts, that depends on where you stand.

If you stand at the beginning or end, your consideration of consequences "to the seventh generation" may seem like a very long time. In the United States, looking back seven generations would take to you to the early days of republic. If an average generation is twenty-five years, seven generations back from today would be one hundred and seventy-five years, and the date would be 1826. A Cherokee alphabet and dictionary is being compiled and the second and third presidents, Thomas Jefferson and John Adams, both die on the 4th of July. Two more generations back would place you squarely in the American Revolution.

Seven generations into the future extends to the year 2176. Given the increasing pace of technological change we experienced in the 20th Century, who would dare to predict the conditions our descendants will meet in the late 22nd Century? To the platitude that "all things change," we can add "even change itself" and balance both with "people are people."

Instead of standing at either end of the time span, however, let's suppose we stand, as we surely do, in the middle. Most Americans in their 50s experience five generations: their grandparents, parents, themselves, their children and grandchildren. By comparison, that seems short-

and-sweet. To experience seven generations, we need only extend our scope of consideration to great-grandparents and great-grandchildren, not such a stretch. One hundred and seventy-five years looks different from the inside.

Another thought that will affect our view of "to the seventh generation" is how we view our preceding generations of ancestors. If we revere and honor them and respect their lives, we deepen our concern for our own actions and their consequences. So-called traditional people are very conservative in this matter: they honor the character and the decisions of their ancestors, reject social experiments, and require satisfactory "proofs" of the benefits of change.

How can we envision generations to come? It's already been suggested that we should remember our children, grandchildren and great-grandchildren and beyond that look to "those faces which come up from the ground to meet us," as the Iroquois still say.

As a practical matter, we have no choice but to consider the seventh-generation concept from our personal perspective. We do have a choice, however, in our attitudes toward the concepts and styles of decision-making. Honor for ancestral actions and consideration of the long-term impacts of decisions will slow the rush of decisions leading to an unknown, but not unknowable, future.

Adding a seventh-generation consideration to the process of consensus decision-making requires participants to stretch their minds in time and space. Imagination would have to be fully employed to both invoke the respected ancestors and to summon generations-to-come. Operating by consensus requires deliberation of at least five options in a continuum, not the simple yes/no switch of an up-or-down vote. Under consensus, "no" can take the form of "no, not for me" or "no, not for anyone here." Similarly, the "yes" option offers "yes, if you want to" and "yes, we will." Between yes and no, there is a neutral position.

Though it may be objected that such a decision-making process will take longer, that argument can be countered by suggesting that such decisions are of higher quality and longer lasting. A decision made using seventh generation criteria and consensus process is more likely to be effective to the seventh generation because of the involvement, trust, and enhanced buy-in of the decision-makers. No one walks away from the decision feeling shut out of the process or as a loser.

The Upshot

Political decisions made with the seventh generation criterion in mind would avoid the pitfalls of current decision-making processes. Such decisions would be made without regard to the immediate gratification of desires for wealth and power and would be, in a sense, anonymous and timeless.

Stephen S. Lewandowski is a graduate of Hamilton College in Clinton, New York with a B.A. in English Literature. He was a Conservation Educator with the Ontario County Soil and Water Conservation District from 1976-2000 and is currently an Environmental Consultant. He has published ten chapbooks of poetry, including his most recent, *O Lucky One*, reviewed in this issue of *Upstream*. He lives in Canandaigua.

"THE MASTER" IN SARANAC LAKE

Stephen Lewandowski

As they did in those days
the consumptives stayed on
through the winter, balancing
time with tourists and campers.
The village fitted itself to their cure—
porches glassed for sun and sleeping—
maximum exposure to healing
mountain light and air.
Tuberculars tried
to outlive the disease.

Far from seeking leisure and ease,
he worked hard at a cure with
long walks in the hills and woods,
returning at dusk to dine with
family and other guests gathered
at the round table built to encircle
the potbelly stove. As they ate
they stretched their slippered feet
toward the heat behind the table.

Up early, he skated on Saranac and
Baker's Pond in a long fur coat.
turning and turning on the clear ice,
his skates cut script and
breath hung in wreaths.

He is remembered in the village
for his rigorous schedule of
exercise, meals, sleeping and writing
and for his great appetites
"constantly smoking,
a cup of coffee always in his hand."

Never before published photograph of RLS in Saranac Lake. From the collection of Stephen Lewandowski.

HOW GOOD SHE WAS

Stephen Lewandowski

I called my teenage classmate Allen
a precarious proposition
in my house because
the phone was mounted
on a wall in the hall
exposed to considerable
traffic through the conversation.
I had my official reasons
for calling Allen
but secretly hoped
for news of my crush
his sister Beth two years
our senior gone on to Cornell
while we were Juniors. On my end
the phone was open to all
the family weather but through
our intimate conversation's flow—
not yet bent to learn of Beth—
there came a voice singing in
Allen's home from a record
that his sister had brought
home from college,
"Who is that?" I asked,
"So we'll go no more a-roving
 So late into the night" sang
the voice of Joan Baez.

LATE NAP

Stephen Lewandowski

For Chip Schramm, 1947-2004

In a jumble of winter lateness—
of day, light and life—
he lay down on the white blanket
covering her bed where she joined him.
His eyes shut, opened, then shut
and stayed closed while
outside the northering sun
turned white sheets covering fields
to scraps left in the shade and
decayed drifts in the hedgerows.

While he slept, she touched his arm,
hip, neck and smiled when he woke
to find her watching him sleep.
In the late winter afternoon,
darkness rose to the precise level
of his eyes as his eyelids fell
until they touched her face.

MENS SCHOOL

Stephen Lewandowski

For Chip, five years later

You my old friend you die once
and we go on thinking of you
in a thousand ways, but you
don't die again- once is enough.

We think of you for years
as we knew you
as you changed and grew, but
now you have stopped changing
so we need to learn to
remember you once & for all.

Perhaps our downfall began
as Freshmen in that French class
where we were in with Upperclassmen
who sat in the back of the room
and smoked their pipes while reading.
We said, that smells good, maybe
we should try that and we did,
later our worldly professor remarked
"It makes the room smell
like a French whorehouse."
How could we know? We were just boys
out to impress the Upperclassmen
putting our heads together
to know the pleasure of
hearing French coming from
our mouths in wreaths of smoke,
smoking our pipes together through
a mild haze from the back of the room.

The Beginning of the Season

Charles "Chip" Schramm

They play five games
and then they decide
who has first ups.
I believe I could enjoy
learning that game.

In the outfield
a leaf falls,
the tree adjusts.

Nine men living
from base to base.
A world without
women and poems.

When it comes you cannot stop
the hard edge of imagination.
You make up stories, but they become
your own heart's desire,

& then you have spoken to someone else
not a teammate.

It was in the spring I realized
there were some people I loved
but could not allow close

and some I took great comfort
in having near me
but did not love

and no one else.

Waiting Room, Oncology

Charles "Chip" Schramm

the mother with baby and toddler,
her poor husband over his head as she
follows the doctor in for her chemo.

the kid here for the second time in two years,
the damn thing back on his liver,
a frat brother taking the time to drive them in.

the woman scared out of her mind
who takes every chance to create chaos
until a nurse calms her down
with magic words.

an older man with funny short hair,
the best part of any worthwhile business
I am capable of doing, already
done.

a father accompanied by
his watchful daughter
fussing over him,
a lovely young woman.

but when they call for the blood test,
she's the one who goes,
protected not at all by her beauty

as I am not protected by my jokes,
my abiding love of so many things of this world.

Suburban man in his doorway

Charles "Chip" Schramm

I own the house, I do not want.
Myself, I'd stand here all night long

and watch the snow. I like to feel
a little chill deep in the bones.

My kids kiss off like loony moths.
The wife makes sense. I hope I don't.

I have this thing about the snow.
I light it, and I watch it dance.

I've had one bold thought. If Jenny dreams
tonight, I think she dreams of this.

Charles R. Schramm III was born in Englewood, NJ on January 14, 1947. "Chip" played baseball at and graduated from Hamilton College in 1969 with a degree in English Literature. He married Susan Penrose and lived in Somerville, MA for 40 years while working for MIT. His children are Will and Kathleen. He wrote poetry his whole life but published little. He died at home on January 23, 2005.

Come Fly with Me

Danusha Goska

A used bookstore in lower Manhattan.
The pages were brittle and dull.
They didn't glare like new bleached frocks.
The pressure fingertips exert just to turn them crumbed them.
This – message deliquescing under touch – feels like nothing else,
except maybe melting ice.
You might be their final reader!
A used bookstore in lower Manhattan.
It was a zoo, really, housing species extinct in the wider world:
excellent damsels who give and wait and yearn and yield;
stalwart, swarthy, lowborn lads who claim the final prize;
true sacrifice for the greater cause.
I was 21. Just back from Africa,
where I loved a vexed Yugoslav,
through Mango Rains and the fire of siege.
I was on my way to Asia
where I'd love a limp WASP
omming in thin Himalayan air.
I turned a corner marked: "Fiction, S."
And there stood a pale fat man with a sweet sweaty face
blinking behind dust-specked spectacles.
"Sabatini," I noted.
"Yes," he breathed.
"Scaramouche," I probed.
"Yes!" he vowed, fervor rising.
"Haven't read that," I confessed;
"My favorite is Captain Blood."
"Oh, yes!" he practically swooned.
Our eyes gleamed. We swayed together, shared pirates, galleons, and duels.
And then, fools, my feet moved on –
time crumbled beneath each step – to Asia, where – mind! –
I saw tigers, un-caged, and kissed at the Taj Mahal
and then and ever since missed

the pale fat man
with a book in his hand
in a used bookstore
in lower Manhattan.

The Women of Darfur

Danusha Goska

A Formerly Homeless American Woman Now Asks God for a Job And Thinks about What Those Prayers Mean

When you pray, do you think of the women of Darfur?
Urgent, whispered, oh so concentrated,
you petition the deity for a job, or a parking space, or a negative biopsy result.
In Darfur, horsemen come, kill all the men, rape all the women, and raze the village.
Even the exotic trees, whose spit makes world politics, and coca-cola, are hacked to the ground.
Journalists' dispatches find the fifth page of the paper but the world does not intervene.
Do you think, "God, yes, give me this job, this parking space, and rescue one Darfur woman"?
Do you think, "God, if I wait ten more minutes for a parking space, if I just go back to cleaning houses,
can we make it ten Darfur women?"
Do you realize that you are not hungry?
That you are not so cold that cold is all you register,
a presence hovering just beyond the stance of each word in your sentence,
a vulture, ready, when you fumble just once,
to swoop in and carry off your ability to form a complete thought?
Do you realize that you are not so hot that you can't have any thoughts…
Do you realize that you are not so tired that anything could have you any time it wanted,
any stray microbe, or mugger, or rapist, or wind
could take your lungs, your bowels, your eyes, your purse, your bipedal verticality,
and you could not resist?

Because that's what it could be. Your life. Your life could be islands of consciousness trapped in a matrix of sensations you devote everything to escaping.

Do you realize how lucky you are to wear shoes?

Do you ever just say "Thank you," "Enough about me," "Let's just concentrate on those women in Darfur"?

When you buy a lottery ticket, when you obsess on how much easier Tom Cruise has it,

when you pray, do you think of the women of Darfur?

I Have to Remember

Danusha Goska

I have to remember:
that the wives don't always have the same last names as the husbands,
the most unlikely people can have power,
not to expect anything,
personal ambition is the highest good,
and not to laugh,
or denounce popular lies,
too loudly.

And I have to remember:
how to dance a czardas,
how much sugar goes in makowiec,
how kiszka smells when it's bursting,
that this isn't forever,
and that my grandmother never learned to read.

Danusha Goska, PhD is a teacher, poet and the author of *Bieganski: The Brute Polak Stereotype, Its Role in Polish-Jewish Relations and American Popular Culture*, winner of the 2010 Halecki Award.

Acorn's Card by Stephen Poleskie. Published by Onager Editions, 2011.

Reviewed by Linda C Wisniewski

A credit card, a packaged loaf of bread, and a plastic bag. Three objects representing more than they seem take center stage in Stephen Poleskie's book *Acorn's Card*.

In the title story, a novella, an injured soldier runs away from his base in Alabama during the Vietnam War and hides out for 33 years in his mother's attic. When his mother dies and he must go out into the world to survive, John Acorn faces the confusing and confused country that has moved on without him. He fills out an application for a credit card, the kind we get in the mail almost every week. What happens next is no surprise. He receives a line of credit of $15,000. What he does with the card, which might also serve as a metaphor for playing the cards we are dealt, propels his story forward almost beyond his control.

John Acorn is an immigrant in the modern world. Even though he has been living within it, unseen, he barely speaks the language. Even though he lives his whole life in the same town, when he emerges from hiding, everything is different. The neighbors' houses are gone, replaced by a highway overpass. Voices in his head haunt him, the remnants of his long years carrying on conversations in the attic with imaginary people. As a character, he brings to mind damaged Vietnam veterans who live forgotten lives on the outskirts of society. As a young man, John Acorn sought only a better life, more interesting than his town and community college could provide. What he got was a traumatic helicopter crash, fear and guilt, and a life in hiding. His story left me wondering how many people just like him withdraw from life, people we never see because they live on the edges, just beyond our sight. Poleskie deftly shows us how difficult it can be to recover when our dreams are dashed to the ground.

The second story, "A Loaf of Bread," takes place on a night in an American city when a Polish immigrant plumber picks the wrong way down a one-way street and comes face to face with police corruption. We've heard before of well-educated immigrants who are forced to take jobs in the United States far beneath their abilities. Jan and Magdalena have become citizens of America but in the author's words, "America was still to them a foreign country, where it was not easy to remain yourself and keep your dignity." They try to make friends but nobody is interested in things they want to talk about like mushroom hunting. They both study hard at night to master English, but their own children talk like rappers on MTV.

The story flashes back to Jan's time as a strike organizer in Gdansk during the Solidarity movement. He narrowly escapes capture by the authorities on a tram and soon after flees with Magdalena to America. The tasteless loaf of white bread he buys that fateful night represents his disappointment but also serves as a catalyst for what we hope will be his next step.

The final story, "Flyer Bag", is a whimsical tale of a white plastic grocery bag and its bid for freedom. My writer's hat is off to Stephen Poleskie for taking on the challenge of creating a story from the point of view of this ubiquitous yet worthless part of the 21st century American landscape.

Typographical errors are a slightly distracting flaw in this collection, which could have benefited from another editor's eye. On the whole, *Acorn's Card* is an enjoyable and thought-provoking meditation on life in America. Its layers of meaning should enrich needed conversations about life in our time.

Linda C Wisnieski is a former Amsterdamian who writes and teaches memoir workshops in Bucks County, PA. Her memoir, *Off Kilter*, was published in 2008 by Pearlsong Press. Visit her website at www.Lindawis.com.

Bieganski: The Brute Polak Stereotype, Its Role in Polish-Jewish Relations and American Popular Culture by Danusha Goska. (Boston: Academic Studies Press), 2010.

An Essay Review by Daniel T. Weaver.

As the title of Danusha Goska's book suggests, it deals with two related but distinct subjects. The first, the role of Polish stereotypes in American culture, is hardly controversial. Polish stereotypes have existed during most of American history. During the early days of the American Republic, Polish stereotypes were positive, based on the contributions of men like Casimir Pulaski and Tadeusz Kosciuszko to the American Revolution as well as other members of the Polish nobility that emigrated to America in the early 19th Century. When working class Poles began coming to the United States in droves, the image of Poles changed to that of a brute, a man existing only slightly above the level of an animal.

What is important about Goska's book is how she shows that negative Polish stereotypes, unlike negative stereotypes of other national, racial and ethnic groups, continue to be acceptable in popular American culture with little outcry from the public, except from the Polish-American community. Goska offers several proofs of the continued acceptance of negative Polish stereotypes including examples from the *New York Times*, the *Washington Post*, the popular film *Borat* and Art Spiegelman's Pulitzer Prize winning graphic novel *Maus*, which depicts Poles as pigs. In Chapter Four, "Bieganski in American Cinema," which was published earlier in *The Journal of Popular Culture*, Goska does an admirable job showing negative Polish stereotypes in four immensely popular films: *A Streetcar Named Desire*, *The Deer Hunter*, *The Fugitive* and *The Apartment*.

Except for parts of Chapter One, the first four chapters of the book—in which Goska describes the development of Polish stereotypes in American History and relates incidents of the ongoing acceptance of negative Polish stereotypes in the American press and cinema—are incontrovertible to any fair minded person. However, Chapters Five through Ten, which deal with relations between Poles and Jews and the close relationship between the negative Polish stereotype, Bieganski (a character in *Sophie's Choice* by William Styron) and the negative Jewish stereotype, Shylock, are controversial. The question is whether they are controversial because of real weaknesses in Goska's presentation and arguments or because most of the people who have found this part of the book troubling are generally either Polish or Jewish and perceive either Goska as antisemitic or not Polish enough.

Goska's book raises two troubling questions. First, why when the Germans planned and carried out the Holocaust, do so many people blame Poland instead and have a higher opinion of Germany than Poland? Secondly, why when both Poles and Jews were both victims of Hitler's racist theories, do some from both sides so despise each other?

Hitler's strategic placement of so many labor and death camps in Poland plays a role in the skewed view of Poland's responsibility for the Holocaust. Added to that is Poland's place in the Soviet Bloc during the Cold War. Goska firmly establishes Israel's role in the continuing negative stereotyping of Poles and Poland, but does she go too far in writing an apologia for Poland's collaboration with Germany in the destruction of Poland's Jewish community as one negative review of her book by a Polish-American suggests and as a Jewish-American wrote in the margins of the review copy of this book before telling me he couldn't review it?

I think a fair argument can be made that Goska does go too far in minimizing antisemitism in Poland and in maximizing Polish aid to Jews during the Holocaust, however, it can also be argued that Goska's book is a needed correction to a skewed perception of Polish collaboration during the Holocaust.

In order to be fair about Poland's role in the Holocaust the following must be kept in mind. First, while 3.1 million Polish Jews were killed in the Second World War, two million ethnic Poles were also killed. All Poles, Jews and Gentiles, were victims of Nazi Germany, although a larger percentage of Jews was killed than ethnic Poles, and while Hitler planned for the annihilation of Jews, his plan for Poles, was servitude.

Secondly, if we compare Poland to other Eastern European nations and even Western European nations like France, Poland collaborated much less with the Nazis and put up stronger resistance.

Thirdly, while Hitler and the Nazis were responsible for the Holocaust, they was aided by the indifference of some Western nations to the plight of the Jews and Slavs and the outright collaboration on the part of many nations. The danger of focusing too much attention on anyone but the Nazis being responsible for the Holocaust is that it can alleviate Nazi guilt and make Hitler's victims, in this case both ethnic Poles and Jews, guilty because some from both groups collaborated.

If we focus on the collaborative Pole as being partially responsible for the Holocaust, can we ignore the Jewish police and councils who decide who were going to go to the camps first and helped round them up, putting their own fate off until later? Elie Wiesel says that every Jew is a victim who requires our respect, regardless of any collaboration on his or her part with the enemy. His thesis would include even people like Stella Kubler, a German-Jewish woman who helped the Gestapo round up hundreds of Jews during World War 2 and committed suicide in 1992 (see Wyden, Peter: *Stella*. New York: Simon & Schuster, 1992). It would also include the Jewish kapo in *The Cap: The Price of a Life* by Roman Frister and Hillel Halkin, who brutally and repeatedly raped Frister when he was a young boy in a concentration camp. The kapo was finally murdered by other Jews for his criminal behavior. When Frister's cap was stolen, he stole one from another inmate, which meant the certain death of that inmate because camp rules required one to wear a cap at all times.

If we are to apply Wiesel's standard to ethnic Poles, also victims of Nazi racial policies, then Goska's defense of the behavior of ethnic Poles in World War 2 is supportable to a large degree. Hitler and the Nazi Party are uniquely guilty for the Holocaust. To place ethnic Poles in the same category as the Nazis or even in the same category as Germans who weren't members of the Nazi Party is historical revisionism on the scale of David Irving or worse. On the other hand, to attempt to ignore or minimize any collaboration on the part of the Poles or any other group is also historical revisionism. And we must also not forget that ethnic Poles had fewer restrictions than Polish Jews, which gave them more opportunity to resist and less need to collaborate.

Similarly, the effort to make Nazis a species apart from the rest of us is also historical revisionism. The director of *Shoah*, Claude Lanzmann did not think that photographs of Hitler as a baby, like the one on the cover of *Explaining Hitler* by Ron Rosenbaum (New York: Harper, 1999), should be published because they bestowed humanity on Hitler. But to portray Hitler as anything but a human being is again to put him into a category that is other than us and lulls us to sleep in thinking that we are incapable of being part of such evil. This self-delusion might be comforting, but it is dangerous. It allows scholars to continue to study the Holocaust and tourists to go to Holocaust museums, all the while virtually ignoring genocide in places like Darfur or our own complicity in the genocide of Native Americans or our behavior in Vietnam and Iraq.

Similarly, Daniel Goldenhagen's *Hitler's Willing Executioners: Ordinary Germans and the Holocaust* (New York: Knopf, 1996), places the blame for the Holocaust on some inherent flaw in the German character. Again if we accept that premise, then we can say genocide can't happen here (i.e. United States, Great Britain, Israel, etc.). For those of us who believe that people are essentially the same throughout the world, it can not only happen here, but many of us who think otherwise, might find ourselves in a position where it is difficult not to be a collaborator. Furthermore, history has shown that genocide occurred before and since the Holocaust on virtually every continent.

In Chapters 5-7, Goska presents three theories as to why Poland, rather than Germany, now "bears" the guilt of the Holocaust, and why negative Polish stereotypes continue to persist. The first theory suggests that Jews are suffering an identity crisis and use Poles to identify who the "other" is, so they can identify who they are. The second theory is the Middleman Theory, in which Jews play the role of the middleman in relation to Poles in the same way Korean businessmen played the role of the middleman in the African-

American neighborhoods of Los Angeles, and were the victims of rioting following the police beating of Rodney King in 1992.

The third theory is that people everywhere are looking for a scapegoat for the Holocaust, and, well, Poland is it.

My simple descriptions of these theories, which are not Goska's alone, defy the complexity of the theories and Goska's explanation and analysis. Nevertheless, I can see where Jews might be offended when reading Chapter Six in particular where the Middleman Minority Theory is applied to Polish-Jewish relations. Indeed, it was this chapter that offended my Jewish-American friend who decided not to review the book after reading it. As he wrote in his notes, "In the end this book itself contains many examples of Jewish stereotypes: Jews as middleman moneylenders, etc."

In the final analysis, however, I believe that Goska makes an honest attempt to employ these theories to explain the baffling reputation of Poland as the perpetrator of the Holocaust and the continued acceptance of negative Polish stereotypes in American culture and elsewhere. *Bieganski*, like most pioneering books, will not likely be the definitive work on Polish stereotypes and Polish-Jewish relations, however, it forces the reader to think about issues he or she has not likely been forced to look at.

And it reminds us of Poland's suffering, which the world seems to have forgotten and which is encapsulated in one paragraph in the book.

"John Guzlowski's Polish Catholic grandmother, aunt, and cousin were murdered by Nazis and Ukranians. They raped John's Aunt Sophie and broke her teeth; they stomped his cousin to death. With his bayonet, a Nazi sexually mutilated John's Aunt Genia. John's parents were Nazi slave laborers; his father was in Buchenwald. John was born in a displaced persons camp after World War II; his family immigrated to America." (286)

While every nation, including Poland, must continue to grapple with its role in the Holocaust, other writers must, if they haven't already, force open widely the door that Goska has opened into the world of Polish suffering. Memoirs of Polish resistance and suffering must be written and published. Art, photography and film must be employed to reach those who won't be reached by an academic book. Only by replacing negative images of Poles in the popular imagination with positive images will the negative stereotype of the Pole be erased.

More importantly, however, both Jews and Poles need to think about where they are now, in 2012, as opposed to 1945 or even 1985. Poland must work hard to stamp out any vestiges of antisemitism; and Jews, particularly those from Israel, must not distort Poland's image. And here in the United States, we must struggle against any attempts to denigrate Jews or Poles. Fortunately, there are wise and generous souls from both sides that are already working to improve relationships between these two groups, both of which share a history that is heavily pregnant with sorrow.

Daniel T. Weaver is the owner of the Book Hound in Amsterdam, New York, publisher and editor of *Upstream A Mohawk Valley Journal* and publisher and editor of the online newspaper, *The Mohawk Valley Independent*.

Books of Note

Daniel T. Weaver

O Lucky One. Stephen Lewandowski. (Kanona, NY: Foothills Publishing, 2010).

O Lucky One is Stephen Lewandowski's tenth chapbook in thirty years of writing poetry. The slim volume contains thirty pages of carefully crafted poems which exhibit deep but not maudlin sentiment.

Lewandowski spent twenty-four years with the Soil Conservation Service, and for the past decade has been a consultant specializing in watershed protection. That Lewandowski has spent a good part of his life outdoors, carefully observing everything around him, is evident in his poetry. Nature is an underlying theme in almost every poem, commencing with the first one, "Flowers, Everywhere", which begins:

"To make
the story short,
she stepped on it
and it stung her."

He writes about "the big blue shoulders of distant mountains" and bears at night which "flow like some dark force through the trees." In "Mock Chaconne," he compares the playing of violins to a storm, and in the last poem of the book, the speaker of the poem regrets losing a knife while out digging test holes.

Lewandowski also writes a lot about women in *O Lucky One*. One beautiful poem, "Admiring Secret Admirer," describes two employees impulsively kissing while working over a map on a table. One gets the feeling that it is a sweet, one-time event, the seal of a relationship that has gone beyond just being co-workers but will not go any further. Unfortunately, the italicized postscript to the poem mars it a bit by explaining that both employees were married to other people and that this was just the dream of a middle-aged man.

In more than one poem, Lewandowski brings together nature and women, as in "Stay In Line."

"The day is cool
the bright sun moves
toward its apogee and
close to summer but
the woman before me
at the post office wears
a short white dress
with a peach sweater
thrown over her
shoulders as if
she intends to
bring on the spring
by sheer force of will,
this peach, pink
and white blossom."

O Lucky One is a much deeper book than this brief review can reveal. It is a nearly perfect chapbook. Even the book itself, the physical object, is beautiful. The front cover is illustrated with a work of art, "Fish in the Forest" by Ren Vasiliev. The end pages are an attractive, heavier blue paper, and rather than stapled together, the pages of the book are sewn together with heavy brown thread. The book is an example of what people lose when they sell off their books and resort to reading books on Nooks and Kindles.

Off Kilter A Woman's Journey To Peace With Scoliosis, Her Mother & Her Polish Heritage. **Linda C. Wisniewski. (Nashville, TN: Pearlsong Press, 2008).**

Growing up in Amsterdam, New York was not easy for Linda Wisniewski. Dealing with scoliosis, shyness, an abusive father, an enabling mother, a religion that allowed little room for women, and being Polish in a society where Polish jokes were acceptable were all issues that would take her years to deal with, and *Off Kilter* appears to be part of her therapy. Wisniewski deals with these issues with honesty and a captivating writing style.

Unlike some memoirists whose childhood was unpleasant and who spend the rest of their lives writing books bashing their parents, their religion and the community they were raised in, Wisniewski appears to have come to terms with the past.

Of her mother, whom she had so much difficulty with, she writes, "When I'm sewing, I feel as if I'm standing on her shoulders as she stood on the shoulders of women before us who sewed through the ages, making clothes, making art, making memories. And if only by a thread, I feel connected to my mother."

She describes her truce with the Roman Catholic Church at her father's funeral. "When I walked through the doors a woman of fifty-four, I was no longer mortified. I enjoyed the beauty of the golden-winged angels on the ceiling and the sunlight streaming through the stained glass, and wrapped myself in memories of children's voices reciting prayers, echoing down the years."

About her father, she says, "I don't believe my father's cruelty made me strong, but it does connect me with other damaged beings."

The girl who was afraid of dissension and other people's anger became a woman who would be a teacher, or guide as she says, to other women, who would find her voice in her writing, and that she has done in *Off Kilter*.

Wisniewski's Polish heritage has become something to celebrate, not be ashamed of. Only her scoliosis is still with her;

and in *Off Kilter*, it becomes a metaphor for her life of which she writes, "My back has been twisted by scoliosis since I was thirteen. My body and my life have always been a little off kilter."

Off Kilter is one of those memoirs I wish I had written, but I am not Polish, a woman, nor do I have scoliosis. On the other hand, *Off Kilter* provides a yardstick, unlike the broken Carpetland yardstick that belongs to Linda's mother, by which aspiring memoirists can measure their work. More importantly, the book combines great storytelling with inspiration for the reader who has a challenging life to continue to struggle and grow.

Diary of a Replacement Soldier: One Man's Remembrance of the Last Days of World War Two in Europe. **(Xlibris Corporation, 2011).**

Former Amsterdamian George Tralka's memoir, *Diary of a Replacement Soldier. One Man's Remembrance of the Last Days of World War Two in Europe*, begins appropriately on December 7, 1941 when he was listening to a radio program at his home at 1 James Street, and an announcer interrupted to say that the Japanese had bombed Pearl Harbor. The next day while delivering the *Schenectady Gazette*, Tralka stopped at the Reid Hill Pharmacy at the corner of Reid and Hibbard Streets to get warm and heard President Roosevelt's famous "Day of Infamy" speech.

The early part of Tralka's memoir reveals a lot about his family and Amsterdam as well as his desire to get into the military. Tralka's father emigrated to the United States from Galicia in Poland by way of Brazil. He lived in several places in the United States and was a Professor of Music at Alliance College in Pennsylvania and first violinist in the Erie Pennsylvania Symphony before moving to Amsterdam, NY. In Amsterdam, the elder Tralka served as organist at St. Stanislaus Church, gave music lessons and sold traditional Christmas wafers door to door to supplement his income.

Tralka's reminiscences of his father are brief—too brief. One wants to know more about him and his mother, particularly since Tralka tells us his father typed out a memoir of his own on a Polish typewriter in response to the call of a Polish language newspaper for immigrants to record their American experiences for posterity.

Tralka's memories of Amsterdam are scanty as well, which is understandable as that is not the aim of his book, but again, the reader, especially the reader from Amsterdam, wants to read more because what Tralka does include about his time in Amsterdam—his descriptions of the Kansas Restaurant, Brownies and the Regent Theatre, for example—leads the reader to conclude that an extended memoir about Amsterdam would be a valuable contribution to the history of the city.

One anecdote Tralka relates that I had never heard before had to do with suspicions aroused by anti-German sentiment during World War 2. The German Lutheran Church on Guy Park Avenue was suspected by some of its neighbors of secretly broadcasting by short wave transmission to Berlin from its copper plated steeple that doubled as an antenna. Of course, the story was not true.

Tralka was still a student at St. Mary's Institute when World War 2 broke out and was not able to get into the military until April of 1944. He missed his own graduation to get into the war and forgot to tell his Senior Prom date that he couldn't make it to the prom.

Most of Tralka's book focuses on the wartime experiences of a typical G.I.—many of them similar in nature to other G.I. memoirs. I have read dozens of these—however, Tralka's is the first I have read by a replacement soldier—a soldier replacing another one who was killed—at the end of the war. A replacement soldier had the unenviable job of trying to become part of a tight knit group that had been together for a long while. Tralka's memoir records the movement of American troops across Germany at the end of the war, thus adding to our overall understanding of that period of the war. Tralka also remained in Germany for awhile after the war, until his allergies got so bad during the blooming German countryside in June of 1945, he was sent home.

Tralka ends his memoir telling how he went to college under the G.I. Bill and became a doctor.

Tralka's memoir is an honest, unassuming account of his life and wartime experiences. It is illustrated by numerous photographs. Tralka's own hand drawn illustrations, done during the war, add to the book's charm. While his his account of his time in Amsterdam is brief, the book is worth reading for that alone. And, of course, if you are a World War 2 buff, it is doubly worth reading.

Upstream is supported solely by The Book Hound. Please support The Book Hound in order to keep *Upstream* going.

The Book Hound
16 E. Main St.
1st Floor
Amsterdam, NY 12010
518 842-7504

Hours
Tues-Fri Noon-5
Sat 11-3

www.thebookhound.net

The Book Hound is a used and antiquarian bookstore with reasonably priced books in all categories. Our prices are generally less than the lowest priced booksellers on the internet.

While The Book Hound stocks books in all categories, our specialties are New York State books, American History, Children's books, religious books and non-fiction.

Additional copies of *Upstream,* as well as many of the books mentioned in it, can be ordered from The Book Hound or on our website www.thebookhound.net. Check out *Upstream's* blog at www.upstreamjournal.wordpress.com.

The Book Hound also publishes the *Mohawk Valley Independent* at www.mohawkvalleyindependent.com.

Made in the USA
Charleston, SC
22 April 2012